R·O·S·E·S

GARDEN GUIDES

THE AMERICAN GARDEN ASSOCIATION

R·O·S·E·S

GARDEN GUIDES

DEREK FELL

SMITHMARK

A FRIEDMAN GROUP BOOK

This edition published in 1992 by SMITHMARK Publishers Inc.,
16 East 32nd Street, New York, NY 10016.

ISBN 0-8317-6938-6

THE AMERICAN GARDEN ASSOCIATION GARDEN GUIDES: ROSES
was prepared and produced by
Michael Friedman Publishing Group, Inc.
15 West 26th Street
New York, NY 10010

Editor: Dana Rosen
Art Director: Jeff Batzli
Designer: Tanya Ross-Hughes
Photography Editor: Christopher C. Bain
Production: Jeanne Kaufman

Typeset by Bookworks Plus
Color separations by Bright Arts Pte. Ltd.
Printed and bound in Hong Kong by Leefung-Asco Printers Ltd.

SMITHMARK Books are available for bulk purchase for sales promotion and
premium use. For details write or call the manager of special sales,
SMITHMARK Publishers Inc., 16 East 32nd Street, New York, NY 10016;
(212) 532-6600.

All photographs © Derek Fell 1992

Acknowledgments

The author wishes to thank Peggy Fisher for help with research, Kathy Nelson for help with typing the manuscript, Wendy Fields for help with picture selections, and Carolyn Heath for help with styling some of the floral compositions.

CONTENTS

ROSES: THE FLORAL EMBLEM

INTRODUCTION

Botanically speaking, all roses are members of the large plant family Rosaceae, which also includes blackberries, apples, and even strawberries among its distinguished members. The rose is classified as a woody plant, as opposed to an herbaceous plant, because it develops a durable woody cell structure rather than a soft stem like many annuals, perennials, and flowering bulbs.

The rose is an extremely versatile plant and has been cultivated in flower gardens for thousands of years. Indeed, there are pottery fragments that suggest a rose garden was cultivated in Greece around the year 5000 B.C. Undoubtedly, what induced early civilizations to grow the rose was its beauty and fragrance.

A big stimulus to the popularity of roses in gardens was the interest in collecting these beautiful flowers held by France's Empress Josephine. She collected about 250 varieties, commissioned the talented botanical illustrator, Redouté, to paint them, and encouraged French nurserymen to develop new varieties. The success of French rose growers encouraged other European countries, particularly England, and soon North American nurserymen were involved in the production and breeding of roses. It was an American nurseryman, Mr. Robert Pyle, who named the famous Peace rose, which was developed by the French rose breeder Meilland.

Today, roses come in many distinct forms (the classification system used today is explained in more detail on page 9). However, regardless of official nomenclature, there are roses that sprawl over the ground (such as the Memorial rose), creating a ground-cover effect, and roses that can grow tall to amazing heights (such as the Cherokee rose). There are roses noted for strong fragrance, roses that grow dense and mounded like a shrub, roses that can be pruned to look like a small tree, and tiny miniatures suitable for growing in pots. There are even wild species of roses that produce attractive ornamental fruit with an edible, vitamin-rich skin that is tasty raw or made into jelly.

The purpose of this book is to present approximately two hundred of the most important roses that are under cultivation throughout the world. Some are star-quality hybrid tea roses with the huge, high-centered blooms favored by floral arrangers; others may be old garden varieties that are still cherished for their fragrance or for another particular reason.

BOTANICAL NOMENCLATURE

Though most modern roses are hybrids and are referred to by their modern classifications, such as hybrid tea and hybrid floribunda, a vast number of old garden roses and wild species are identified by botanical names. For example *Rosa banksiae* describes a wild yellow rose native to China. The first name, *Rosa*, describes the genus, or family, and the second identifies the specific species. Sometimes a third name appears in a rose listing, such as *Rosa banksiae* 'Alba', identifying a white-flowered form, called a variety. When a variety is the result of plant breeding, the variety is sometimes called a cultivar (short for "cultivated variety"), but the modern tendency is to use variety to describe both true varieties and cultivars.

When a rose is the result of hybridizing, it often has an × in its name, signifying a cross, such as *Rosa × harisonii*. This symbol identifies a hybrid between two or more species.

In describing rose flowers, the term "single-flowered" means the flower is made up of a single row of petals, such as the hybrid 'Nevada'. The term "semidouble-flowered" means the bloom has two rows of petals, such as the white rose of York; "double-flowered" means the bloom has more than two rows of petals, like the old garden rose 'Chapeau de Napoleon', which might have more than two hundred petals in each flower head.

OBTAINING ROSES

The most convenient place to obtain roses is your local garden center or a plant nursery that specializes in roses. You will find that the selection varies widely, with some retail outlets offering as few as three varieties—a red, a pink, and a yellow—all hybrid teas. They may be offered bare-root, with their roots washed clean of soil but kept moist by a packing of damp sphagnum moss, sawdust, or newspaper and protected by a clear plastic wrapper. Or they may be offered potted, with the roots growing in soil. When purchasing, give a potted plant a gentle tug just to make sure that the roots are really growing in the soil and that a bare-root plant has not simply been inserted into a pot with potting soil loosely packed around it for the sake of appearances. Potted plants generally fetch more than the bare-root kind.

Another way to buy roses is from a mail-order catalog. Many companies produce colorful books with detailed descriptions, vivid pictures, and a large selection to choose from. You can usually find the catalogs offered free or for a small charge in the advertising pages of garden magazines. Some catalog houses may specialize in a particular kind of rose—for example, "all miniatures" or "old garden roses." Some catalogs will even offer different grades, such as #1½, and #2 grade. It almost always pays to choose the #1 grade.

You may also want to search out rose gardens in your area. Botanical gardens generally have a rose collection, and in the spring they may offer for sale some of the scarce varieties. In any event, it helps to visit rose gardens in your area to see what kinds of roses do well and which ones appeal to you. Sometimes you will discover that the rose you admire has a rating, such as a gold medal from the National Rose Society of Great Britain, or a numerical rating from the American Rose society.

RATINGS

The American Rose Society rates roses from 1 to 10. The ratings are based on a sampling among its national membership. The society considers 10 to be perfect (though no rose has ever been rated so high); 9.0 and above is outstanding; 8.0 and above is excellent; 7.0 and above is fair; and anything below 6.0 is not worth growing in their opinion. Some chapters of the American Rose Society have their own rating systems, so it is generally best to seek a local rating if you live in an unusual climatic area.

ALL-AMERICAN ROSE AWARDS

Some roses are tagged with an All-America Award, meaning they received a special high rating in twenty-three test gardens throughout North America. All-America rose selections are announced each year in spring, although there have been years when no rose was considered worthy of an award.

CLASSIFICATION OF ROSES

A ROSE FOR ANY PURPOSE

Roses are exceptionally versatile and make useful landscaping plants. They combine superbly with other perennials and bulbs. Here are the major classes of roses and their landscaping applications.

HYBRID TEAS

The most popular rosebush, hybrid teas are generally tall and stately with large, well-formed blooms. They are commonly used as single specimen plantings or as the featured plants in a mixed bed of roses. Many are highly fragrant.

GRANDIFLORAS

Grandifloras are similar to hybrid teas and often classified as hybrid teas (particularly in England, where the grandiflora class is not recognized). The flowers tend to be carried in clusters and have a greater mass of color than the typical hybrid tea. The plants are taller, the stems shorter, but they are still suitable for cutting. Hybrid teas and grandifloras form excellent borders and are effective massed in beds, used individually as accents, or placed in front of picture windows.

FLORIBUNDAS

Floribundas are now the second-largest class of roses. They are shorter than hybrid teas and bloom heavily, producing clusters of flowers from June until frost. Their short height makes them ideal for borders, for lining walks, or for combining with hybrid teas in a bed.

CLIMBING ROSES

Vigorous and easy to grow, climbing roses provide generous displays of bloom and add dramatic highlights to your landscape. They can lend interest to a blank wall or be trained on fences and latticework.

TREE ROSES

A sturdy, straight cane gives tree roses a magnetic elegance, whether they are in containers, lining a walk, or simply used to add height to an existing rose bed. Tree roses are always guaranteed to attract a viewer's attention.

MINIATURES

These short bushes, with their small, perfectly formed blooms, are ideal for gardens with limited space: small areas; and deck, patio, or porch containers.

SHRUB AND OLD GARDEN ROSES

Shrub and old garden roses are especially versatile as landscaping plants whether you're looking for an eye-catching hedge, a colorful border, bright color accents for blank walls and rock gardens, or container plants for the deck or patio. Many old garden roses with heavy fragrances are classified as shrub roses.

SPECIES ROSES

Species roses are wild types. Some are shrublike, such as *R. rugosa*; others are rambling, such as *R. laevigata*. These wild roses are good for naturalized settings, such as the edge of a meadow.

PLANTING ROSES

Whether you are planting bare-root or potted plants, it's a good idea to soak the entire plant for three to four hours in lukewarm water and to plant outdoors in the spring after danger of freezing weather has passed. If you cannot plant your roses immediately upon arrival, store them in a cool place, 34° to 50°F (1° to 10°C).

The longer your growing season, the larger your rose bushes will grow, with your amount of available space the controlling factor. Usually, the closer together you plant your bushes, the more pruning you must do to keep them from suffocating.

To create a massed bedding effect, hybrid teas, floribundas, and grandifloras should be spaced at least 3 feet (.9m) apart. Tree roses should be spaced 3 to 5 feet (.9 to 1.5m) apart. Miniatures, being a good deal smaller than even floribundas, can be spaced 10 to 18 inches (25 to 46cm) apart, depending on the variety.

Dig planting holes 18 inches (46cm) deep and add lots of humus. The best soil for roses is a humus-rich, fertile loam. If your soil is too sandy or clayish, add lots of compost, peat, or leaf mold.

STEP-BY-STEP PLANTING FOR A BARE-ROOT ROSE

1. Dig a hole large enough for the roots and form a firm mound of soil in the hole. The top of the mound should be high enough that the bud union (the knob where the canes join the main stalk) is just above ground level when the soil settles.

2. Now give the plant a light haircut. Prune the canes back to about 8 inches (20cm), making the cuts 1/4 inch (6mm) above an outside bud. Remove any broken canes or roots and trim the roots so they are all approximately the same length. Spread the roots carefully and place the plant on the rounded top of the mound. Check the height of the bud union.

3. Work your prepared soil around the roots and firm it with your hands, taking care not to damage any roots. Add more soil and firm. Continue until you can safely firm the soil with your foot to within 2 inches (5cm) of the top of the hole.

4. Fill the remainder of the hole with water — 2 or 3 gallons (8 or 11l)—and allow it to soak in. Check the bud union again.

5. Mound the remaining soil with compost, peat moss, or sawdust around the plant until the canes are covered in order to prevent them from drying out before growth starts. When growth begins, in about ten days, carefully remove the mound of organic material. Loosen or remove the plant name tag so it does not constrict the cane growth. When vigorous growth has started, apply a rose plant food according to the manufacturer's directions.

If your rose came in a pot, dig a hole slightly larger than the pot or container. Carefully remove the plant and soil ball from the pot. Set it in the hole with the bud union above soil level. Pour soil mix around the ball until the hole is about three-quarters full. Fill the remainder with water and allow it to soak in. Finish filling the soil and firm it gently so as not to break the soil ball. Water frequently because the soil ball will tend to dry out quickly until the plant becomes well established. Fertilize when vigorous growth starts.

AFTER PLANTING

The most important aftercare for your roses consists of watering, fertilizing, spraying, and pruning.

Regardless of where you live and what the climate is, your plants require attention in each of these four areas. However, your climate, the length of the growing season in your area, and soil conditions do play a significant role in rose growing. Therefore, the following advice is general, and you are advised to consult with successful rose growers in your area.

WATERING

If you were to dig up an established rose garden, you would be amazed at the size of the fine feeder root systems as compared with the tops of the plants. This root system is very efficient as long as the plant receives adequate water. A good rule of thumb to follow would be five gallons (19l) per plant per watering. You should always be sure not to let a week go by without watering your roses, unless you experience natural rainfall.

FERTILIZING

Although roses thrive on balanced fertilizers high in phosphorus and minerals, feeding in early spring and again in midsummer is usually adequate. Too much fertilizer can reduce the vibrancy of the color and late fertilization can even result in a reduction of hardiness.

SPRAYING

Every area has its share of fungus problems and its own special insect pests that attack rose plants. Control these by applying rose food with an added systemic pesticide or by spraying. The best time to spray is in the early morning or within twenty-four hours after watering. Use a spray recommended by your garden store; generally, you'll find a rose spray formulated to handle both fungus problems and pests. Spray all over the plant and on the ground around it. Read the label, for different brands differ in their rates of application. Some roses are naturally resistant to pests and fungus disease.

PRUNING

Pruning is done to keep the plant healthy and to produce top-grade blooms. Obviously, you will remove dead or dying canes. Also, you should limit the number of canes to those that are the healthiest, remove overcrowded growth in the center of the plant, and control the height and shape. Cutting your blooms is a beneficial part of the process.

COMMON ROSE PROBLEMS

APHIDS

Soft-bodied red, brown, or green insects, usually wingless, about 1/8 inch (3mm) long, found mostly on new growth near developing buds. Prefer cooler weather in spring or autumn.

SYMPTOMS Curled leaves and/or malformed flowers. Clusters of insects on buds and canes.

REMEDY One of the most easily eliminated garden pests. Hose off three times, once every other day. Hose in the morning, allowing leaves to dry in the sun—wet foliage encourages mildew.

BEETLES

Metallic brown-, black-, or green-bodied insects usually found devouring the leaves and the petals.

SYMPTOMS Tissue of the leaves has been eaten, leaving only the skeleton. Unopened flower buds have been devoured, distorting their shape.

REMEDY Hand pick beetles or spread a cloth or paper beneath the plant, shake it, pick up the cloth, and destroy beetles. Or spray with a commercial insecticide when beetles are actively feeding on roses.

BLACKSPOT

Dark black spots on the leaves. Common in rainy weather.

SYMPTOMS Bottom leaves turn yellow and fall from the plant during periods of high infection.

REMEDY Keep foliage dry by watering roots with wand or soaker. If you must wet foliage, do it early in the day so it dries by night. Apply fungicides at five-day intervals, or according to label directions.

BOTRYTIS BLIGHT

A fungus usually occurring during cold, wet weather.

SYMPTOMS Brown spots on petals. In severe cases, blooms will become brown. Blooms may not open. As ends turn brown, light brown spores are produced. Dieback progresses downward from the tips.

REMEDY Spray with a general-purpose rose fungicide.

CANKER

Sometimes confused with botrytis, canker is caused by a parasitic fungus that enters through wounds or dying tissue.

SYMPTOMS Lesions in woody tissue of cane, poor growth, dead growth above affected area.

REMEDY Prune out and dispose of all affected areas, cutting well below canker with shears dipped in alcohol or bleach after each cut.

CATERPILLARS AND WORMS

These pests chew holes in flower buds and leaves or skeletonize leaves.

REMEDY Apply *Bacillus thuringiensis,* a nontoxic remedy harmful only to caterpillars. Can also use a number of insecticidal sprays.

POWDERY MILDEW

Gray to white powdery growth that attacks new leaves and buds, especially during periods of high humidity.

SYMPTOMS Leaves fold at midrib. White powdery material on buds and leaves. Blooms fail to open.

REMEDY Water wash can be tried first. If this fails, you can try a general-purpose rose fungicide. Avoid evening watering—wet foliage overnight encourages mildew.

RUST

The same conditions that cause blackspot also produce rust, which shows up as rust-colored patches located on the foliage. Treatment is the same as for blackspot (see page 17).

SPIDER MITES (RED SPIDER)

Visible to the unaided eye as reddish specks, these tiny pests suck out the sap of the foliage. They spread quickly and favor the heat of midsummer.

SYMPTOMS Underside of plant's bottom leaves appear to be covered with fine grains of sand. Leaves turn yellow and fall off. Sometimes webs are visible.

REMEDY Spray leaves—especially undersides—with a fine spray of a commercial insecticide that specifically lists mites. Repeat applications are usually necessary to interrupt the breeding cycle; follow label directions.

THRIPS

Quick-moving, slender, light brown insects, less than ⅛ inch (3mm) long.

SYMPTOMS Blooms are discolored with white or brown streaks; frequently they fail to open. To see if your roses have thrips, gently give the opening bud a quick squeeze and look inside the petals for fast-moving insects.

REMEDY Difficult to control except by a commercial spray used on a regular basis, according to label directions.

CONTAINER PLANTINGS

Roses can be grown in containers, so they can be enjoyed by the apartment and condominium dweller who has a balcony or entrance porch that receives sufficient sunlight, and by the inner city dweller having limited garden space.

Containers must be of adequate size and drain well. A rule-of-thumb measurement is 24 inches (61cm) in diameter, 14 inches (36cm) deep, other than for miniature roses, which require 8 by 6 inches (20 by 15cm). If more than one plant is planned in a planter box, adequate space must be provided between plants (see planting guide, page 13). Two other factors, winter weather and the plant's thirst requirements, must also be considered before launching a container rose garden. In areas of medium to severe winters, it will be necessary to guard your container roses against freezing. In areas where the temperature drops to 20°F or lower, roses in small containers can be dug into your garden up to the lip of the container and retrieved in the spring.

HELPFUL HINTS FOR THE BEGINNING ROSE GROWER

DISBUDDING

Disbudding is the process of reducing the number of buds on the hybrid tea rose for large, exhibition-quality flowers. Remove all side buds on each stem while they are very small, leaving only the central or terminal bud on each stem. Rub out the side buds with your finger as soon as they can be removed without damaging the central bud. This allows the plant to produce a bloom of superior size and quality.

SUN OR SHADE

Roses love at least five hours of sun a day and will sit and pout if planted in swampy spots. If a rose fails to bloom, chances are it doesn't have enough sunlight.

SOIL

Add organic matter to sandy or clayish soil. In order of desirability are dried or rotted manure from dairies or stables; thoroughly composted leaves and peat moss; and fine bark dust (but not sawdust unless it has been composted).

THE ROSES

ACCENT

TYPE: Floribunda

ORIGIN: Hybridized by William Warriner (U.S.A.) and introduced by Jackson & Perkins (U.S.A.) in 1977. A cross between Marlena and an unnamed seedling.

RATING: Not rated by the American Rose Society.

HABIT: 3 to 4 feet (.9 to 1.2m). Bushy, compact growth. Leaves are small, leathery, dark.

FLOWERS: Cardinal red, double; 25 petals open out flat to 2½ inches (6.5cm) in diameter. Free-flowering. Slightly fragrant.

USES: Mass in beds and mixed borders.

AMBASSADOR

TYPE: Hybrid tea

ORIGIN: Hybridized by the House of Meilland (France) under the name Meinuzeton and introduced into North America by Conard-Pyle (U.S.A.) in 1979. A cross between an unnamed seedling and Whiskey Mac.

RATING: ARS 6.9.

HABIT: 3 to 4 feet (.9 to 1.2m). Leaves are glossy, dark green.

FLOWERS: Orange-red with golden yellow on reverse, fully double with 33 petals that form a 4-inch (10cm) diameter cup shape when fully open.

USES: Mixed beds and borders. Good for cutting.

AMBER QUEEN

TYPE: Floribunda

ORIGIN: Hybridized and introduced by the House of R. Harkness (Great Britain) in 1984. A cross between Southampton and Typhoon.

RATING: ARS 7.5. All-America Rose Selection 1984; Rose of the Year Award Great Britain 1984.

HABIT: 3 feet (.9m). Low, bushy growth. Leaves are large, glossy, dark green or coppery red.

FLOWERS: Plump bronze buds open out into large, orange, cup-shaped, fully double blooms with 40 petals. Borne in clusters of 3 to 7, up to 4 inches (10cm) across. Fragrant.

USES: Massing in beds and mixed borders. Good for cutting.

AMERICA

TYPE: Climbing rose

ORIGIN: Hybridized by William Warriner (U.S.A.) and introduced by Jackson & Perkins (U.S.A.) in 1976. A cross between Fragrant Cloud and Tradition.

RATING: ARS 8.9; All-America Award 1976.

HABIT: 9 to 12 feet (2.7 to 3.7m). Vigorous tall growth; good disease resistance. Leaves are medium-size, semiglossy, medium green.

FLOWERS: Coral-salmon, fully double, high-centered, up to 4½ inches (11cm) across. Continuous flowering. Lightly fragrant.

USES: Good to cover arbors and train up trellis.

AMERICAN BEAUTY

TYPE: Old garden rose

ORIGIN: Hybridized by Ledechaux (France) in 1875 and introduced by Field Bros. (U.S.A.) in 1886. Parents unknown. Classified as a hybrid perpetual.

RATING: ARS 7.7.

HABIT: Up to 6 feet (1.8m). Vigorous, erect growth; hardy, disease-resistant. Canes are almost thornfree; leaves are glossy, dark green.

FLOWERS: Deep pink, double, high-centered, up to 6 inches (15cm) across; resembles a hybrid tea. Fragrant.

USES: Popular greenhouse rose, especially in Europe where it is known as Madame Ferdinand Jamain. Also good for garden display.

AMERICAN PILLAR

TYPE: Climbing rose

ORIGIN: Hybridized by Van Fleet (U.S.A.) in 1902 and introduced by Conard & Jones (U.S.A.) in 1908. A cross between *R. wichuraiana* and *R. setigera* onto an unnamed red hybrid perpetual.

RATING: Not rated by the American Rose Society.

HABIT: Up to 20 feet (6m). Vigorous, tall growth; hardy and disease-resistant, though subject to mildew in warm climates. Thorny canes have medium-size, leathery green leaves.

FLOWERS: Carmine-pink with a white eye, single, up to 2½ inches (6.5cm) across, held in clusters. Prolific flowering in spring, though no repeat bloom, and no fragrance.

USES: Excellent coverage of arbors, gazebos; training along walls.

ANGEL FACE

TYPE: Floribunda

ORIGIN: Hybridized by Swim & Weeks (U.S.A.) and introduced by Conard-Pyle (U.S.A.) in 1968. A cross between Circus and Lavender Pinocchio onto Sterling Silver.

RATING: ARS 8.2; All-America Award 1969; American Rose Society Jack Cook Medal 1971.

HABIT: Up to 3 feet (.9m). Bushy growth; hardy and disease-resistant. Thorny canes bear leathery, dark green leaves.

FLOWERS: Lavender-mauve, double, up to 4 inches (10cm) across, borne in clusters. Fragrant.

USES: One of the best so-called "blue" roses. Good for massing; admired by floral arrangers.

APOLLO

TYPE: Hybrid tea

ORIGIN: Hybridized and introduced by Armstrong Roses (U.S.A.) in 1971. A cross between High Time and Imperial Gold. Also known as Armolo.

RATING: ARS 4.8; All-America Rose Selections 1972.

HABIT: 4 to 5 feet (1.2 to 1.5m). Vigorous, bushy growth. Leaves are large, glossy, dark green.

FLOWERS: Long, pointed buds open out into 5-inch (13cm), bright yellow, fragrant flowers.

USES: Mixed beds and borders. Good for cutting.

APOTHECARY'S ROSE

TYPE: Old garden rose

ORIGIN: Often listed as *R. gallica officinalis*. Also commonly called the Red Rose of Lancaster. Cultivated before 1600. *R. gallica versicolor,* a striped sport, often listed as *R. mundi versicolor*, is also known as the Apothecary's Rose and is more commonly grown.

RATING: ARS 9.2 (highest rating of any old garden rose).

HABIT: Up to 4 feet (1.2m). Vigorous, bushy growth; hardy and disease-resistant. Canes bear prickles rather than true thorns; leaves dark green.

FLOWERS: Deep pink or pink-and-white bicolored; up to 4 inches (10cm) across, with a flattened, semidouble form and prominent golden yellow stamens. Mostly spring-blooming. Enchanting fragrance. Round red hips in autumn.

USES: Popular accent in informal cottage-style gardens, also herb gardens. Creates a dense hedge.

AQUARIUS

TYPE: Grandiflora

ORIGIN: Hybridized and introduced by Armstrong Roses (U.S.A.) in 1971. From a complicated cross involving Charlotte Armstrong, Contrast, Fandango, Floradora, and World's Fair.

RATING: ARS 7.2; Gold Medal Geneva 1970; All-America Rose Selection 1961.

HABIT: 3 to 4 feet (.9 to 1.2m). Upright, bushy growth; disease-resistant. Leaves are large, leathery, dark green.

FLOWERS: Pink bicolored, double, high-centered bloom. Continuous flowering. Slightly fragrant.

USES: Mixed beds and borders. Good for cutting.

ARIZONA

TYPE: Grandiflora

ORIGIN: Hybridized by the House of Weeks (U.S.A.) and introduced by Conard-Pyle (U.S.A.) in 1975. A cross between Golden Scepter and Fred Howard onto Golden Rapture.

RATING: ARS 6.2. All-America Award 1975.

HABIT: Up to 6 feet (1.8m). Vigorous, upright, bushy growth. Leaves are glossy, leathery, dark green.

FLOWERS: Golden bronze, double, high-centered, up to 4½ inches (11cm) across. Strongly fragrant.

USES: Mass planting in island beds. Excellent for cutting.

AUTUMN GOLD

TYPE: Hybrid tea

ORIGIN: Hybridized by the House of Weeks (U.S.A.) and introduced in 1969. A cross between unnamed seedlings.

RATING: ARS 6.2.

HABIT: 4 to 5 feet (1.2 to 1.5m). Upright growth. Leaves are leathery, glossy, dark green.

FLOWERS: High-pointed buds open out into butterscotch yellow, globular, fully doub. blooms, up to 4 inches (10cm) across, with 42 petals.

USES: Mixed beds and borders. Good for cutting.

BAHIA

TYPE: Floribunda

ORIGIN: Hybridized by Dr. W. E. Lamments (U.S.A.) and introduced by Armstrong Roses (U.S.A.) in 1974. A cross between Rumba and Tropicana.

RATING: Not rated by the American Rose Society. All-America Rose Selection 1974.

HABIT: 3 to 4 feet (.9 to 1.2m). Leaves are glossy, dark green. Upright, bushy growth.

FLOWERS: Rich orange, double blooms up to 3 inches (7.5cm) across. Spicy fragrance.

USES: Mixed beds and borders. Good for cutting.

BALLERINA

TYPE: Shrub rose

ORIGIN: Developed by Bentall (England) in 1937. Classified as a hybrid musk rose of unknown parentage.

RATING: Not rated by the American Rose Society.

HABIT: 4 feet (1.2m). Arching, fountainlike growth; hardy and disease-resistant. Slender, lightly thorned canes bear glossy, light green leaves.

FLOWERS: Pink, single, blooming in clusters. Individual flowers measure 1 inch (2.5cm) across. Petal edges deep pink; white center surrounds a crown of yellow stamens. Heaviest bloom in spring, some repeat blooms. Light fragrance.

USES: Popular for grafting to create a weeping rose "standard" (tree-form rose). Good accent for mixed shrub borders.

BARON GIROD DE L'AIN

TYPE: Old garden rose

ORIGIN: Introduced by Reverchon (France) in 1897. A sport of Eugene Furst. Classified as a hybrid perpetual.

RATING: ARS 7.1.

HABIT: Up to 5 feet (1.5m). Bushy, erect growth; hardy and disease-resistant. Thorny canes bear semiglossy dark green leaves.

FLOWERS: Dark red with petal tips frosted white. Double form up to 4 inches (10cm) across. Resembles a peony. Highly fragrant.

USES: Hybrid perpetuals help bring an old-fashioned look to informal cottage-style gardens. Their popularity peaked in the 1800s, when over three thousand varieties were introduced. They bloom best when nights are cool, predominantly in spring, with a small show again in autumn.

BARONNE PREVOST

TYPE: Old garden rose

ORIGIN: Introduced by 1842. Developed by Desprez (France) and descended from Damask, China, and Bourbon roses. Classified as a hybrid perpetual.

RATING: ARS 7.5.

HABIT: Up to 5 feet (1.5m). Vigorous upright, bushy growth; hardy and disease-resistant. Canes are almost thorn-free, bear semiglossy, dark green leaves.

FLOWERS: Deep rose-pink, with numerous petals that seem to create a flat, swirling flower head up to 3 inches (7.5cm) across. Predominantly spring-flowering. Heavily scented.

USES: Good shrub accent in collections of old garden roses. Beautiful cut flower.

BEAUTY SECRET

TYPE: Miniature

ORIGIN: Hybridized by R. S. Moore (U.S.A.) and introduced by Sequoia Nurseries (U.S.A.) in 1965. A cross between Little Darling and Magic Wand.

RATING: ARS 9.3. Award of Excellence America Rose Society 1975.

HABIT: Up to 12 inches (31cm). Dwarf, bushy, compact growth. Leaves are leathery, glossy, green.

FLOWERS: Christmas-red, pointed buds open out into semidouble blooms, up to 1½ inches (4cm) across. Pleasant sweet fragrance.

USES: Flowering pot plant. Popular gift plant at Christmastime. Excellent for edging beds and borders.

BELLE DE CRECY

TYPE: Old garden rose

ORIGIN: Introduced by Roeser (France) prior to 1829. Classified as a Gallica.

RATING: ARS 7.5.

HABIT: Up to 5 feet (1.5m). Vigorous, arching, bushy growth; hardy and disease-resistant. Prickly canes bear dull, dark green leaves.

FLOWERS: Violet, almost purple, double, button-nose blooms up to 3 inches (7.5cm) across. Highly fragrant.

USES: One flower will fill a room with fragrance. Good accent in mixed beds and borders, especially in informal cottage-style gardens.

BETTY PRIOR

TYPE: Floribunda

ORIGIN: Hybridized by Betty Prior (Great Britain) in 1935 and introduced by Jackson & Perkins (U.S.A.) in 1938. A cross between Kirsten Poulsen and an unnamed seedling.

RATING: ARS 8.5. Royal National Rose Society of Great Britain Gold Medal 1935.

HABIT: Up to 4 feet (1.2m). Vigorous, bushy growth; hardy and disease-resistant. Thorny canes bear medium-size, medium green leaves.

FLOWERS: Carmine-pink with white centers, single, up to 3½ inches (9cm) across, borne profusely in clusters. Mostly spring-flowering.

USES: Good accent plant used alone or combined with perennials. Makes an attractive flowering hedge.

BEWITCHED

TYPE: Hybrid tea

ORIGIN: Hybridized by Lammerts (U.S.A.) and introduced by Germain's Roses (U.S.A.) in 1967. A cross between Queen Elizabeth and Tawny Gold.

RATING: ARS 7.0. Gold Medal Portland 1967; All-America Rose Selection 1967.

HABIT: 3 to 4 feet (.9 to 1.2m). Vigorous, bushy growth. Leaves are glossy, dark green.

FLOWERS: Medium pink, large, double flowers with 25 petals, up to 5 inches (13cm) across. Pleasantly fragrant.

USES: Good accent in mixed beds and borders. A superb color for floral arrangements.

BING CROSBY

TYPE: Hybrid tea

ORIGIN: Hybridized by the House of Weeks (U.S.A.) and introduced in 1980. A cross between First Prize and an unnamed seedling.

RATING: ARS 6.5. All-America Award 1981.

HABIT: Up to 4 feet (1.2m). Vigorous, upright, bushy growth. Thorny canes bear leathery, wrinkled, dark green leaves.

FLOWERS: Orange-red, double, up to 4 inches (10cm) across, borne singly. Slightly fragrant.

USES: Massing in beds. Good cut flower in the mature bud stage.

BLAZE

TYPE: Climbing rose

ORIGIN: Hybridized by Kallay (U.S.A.) and introduced by Jackson & Perkins (U.S.A.) in 1932. A cross between Paul's Scarlet and Grüss an Teplitz.

RATING: ARS 7.3. One of the most popular roses for home gardens.

HABIT: Up to 9 feet (2.7m). Vigorous growth; hardy and disease-resistant. Leaves are medium-size, glossy, light green.

FLOWERS: Scarlet, semidouble, cup-shaped, up to 3 inches (7.5cm) across, borne in clusters. Prolific bloom production in spring with sporadic repeat bloom. Slight fragrance.

USES: Training up trellis, along split rail and picket fences. Can be pruned to create a dense, shrubby habit.

BLUE MOON

TYPE: Hybrid tea

ORIGIN: Hybridized by the House of Tantau (Germany) and introduced in 1964. A cross between Sterling Silver and an unnamed seedling.

RATING: ARS 6.9. Gold Medal Rome 1964.

HABIT: 3 to 4 feet. Vigorous, bushy growth; disease-resistant, but needs protection against winterkill. Leaves are glossy, dark green.

FLOWERS: Lilac-blue, double with 40 petals, up to 4 inches (10cm) across. One of the best "blue" roses. Very fragrant.

USES: Mixed beds and borders. Excellent for cutting, especially in the mature bud stage.

BON-BON

TYPE: Floribunda

ORIGIN: Hybridized by William Warringer (U.S.A.) and introduced by Jackson & Perkins (U.S.A.) in 1974. A cross between Bridal Pink and an unnamed seedling.

RATING: Not rated by the America Rose Society. All-American Rose Selection 1974.

HABIT: 3 to 4 feet (.9 to 1.2m). Bushy growth. Leaves are dark green.

FLOWERS: Deep rose-pink petals have white undersides; semidouble, up to 3½ inches (9cm) across. Fragrant.

USES: Mixed beds and borders.

BRANDY

TYPE: Hybrid tea

ORIGIN: Hybridized and introduced by Armstrong Roses (U.S.A.) in 1981. A cross between First Prize and Dr. A. J. Verhage.

RATING: ARS 7.3. All-America Award 1982.

HABIT: Up to 5 feet (1.5m). Stong, upright, bushy growth. Thorny canes bear large, dark green leaves.

FLOWERS: Deep apricot, double, up to 4 inches (10cm) across. Mild tea fragrance.

USES: Massing in beds and borders. Good high, pointed mature bud shape, valued by flower arrangers as "sweetheart" roses.

BROADWAY

TYPE: Hybrid tea

ORIGIN: Hybridized by Anthony Perry (U.S.A.) and introduced by Cooperative Rose Growers (U.S.A.) in 1986. Resulting from a cross between First Prize and Gold Glow with Sutter's Gold.

RATING: ARS 7.1. All-America Rose Selection 1986.

HABIT: 4 feet (1.2m). Vigorous, upright growth. Leaves are semiglossy, dark green.

FLOWERS: Golden yellow suffused with pink; large, high-centered, up to 5½ inches (14cm) across. Flowers in mature bud stage are well-formed, composed of 35 petals. Fragrant.

USES: Mixed beds and borders. Good for cutting.

CAMAIEUX

TYPE: Old garden rose

ORIGIN: Introduced in 1830. Classified as a Gallica.

RATING: ARS 7.5.

HABIT: Up to 5 feet (1.5m). Vigorous, bushy growth. Dark green leaves.

FLOWERS: Deep pink with white stripes, double, camellialike, up to 4 inches (10cm) across. Blooms for up to 6 weeks in spring. Highly fragrant.

USES: Good accent for informal cottage-style gardens. Excellent for cutting and potpourri.

CAMELOT

TYPE: Grandiflora

ORIGIN: Hybridized by Swim & Weeks (U.S.A.) and introduced by Conrad-Pyle (U.S.A.) in 1964. Resulting from a cross between Circus and Queen Elizabeth.

RATING: ARS 7.5. All-America Rose Selection 1965.

HABIT: 5 to 6 feet (1.5 to 1.8m). Vigorous, tall growth; disease-resistant. Leaves are leathery, glossy, dark green.

FLOWERS: Salmon-pink, double, with 48 petals. Cupped, up to 3½ inches (9cm) across, borne in clusters throughout the season. Spicy fragrance.

USES: Suitable for tall, back-of-the-border highlights, training up trellis. Cut flowers last well in water.

CANDY STRIPE

TYPE: Hybrid tea

ORIGIN: Discovered by McCummings (U.S.A.) and introduced by Conard-Pyle (U.S.A.) in 1963. A sport of Pink Peace.

RATING: ARS 6.5.

HABIT: 4 feet (1.2m). Upright growth. Leaves are dark green.

FLOWERS: Deep pink, up to 4½ inches (11.5cm) across, streaked with white or light pink, double. Similar in appearance to Candystick, which is a sport of Better Times. Slight fragrance.

USES: Not as free-flowering as other hybrid teas. Mostly grown as a curiosity and for flower arrangements.

CARDINAL DE RICHELIEU

TYPE: Old garden rose

ORIGIN: Introduced by Laffay (France) in 1840, though its true origin may be Holland. Possibly a cross between a Gallica and a China rose. Classified as a Gallica hybrid.

RATING: ARS 7.1.

HABIT: Up to 4 feet (1.2m). Bushy, compact growth; hardy and disease-resistant. Smooth canes bear small, glossy, dark green leaves.

FLOWERS: Purple with a white button center, double, cupped, up to 2 inches (4cm) across, borne in clusters. Slightly fragrant.

USES: Accent in informal cottage-style gardens.

CAREFREE BEAUTY

TYPE: Shrub rose

ORIGIN: Hybridized by Dr. G. J. Buck of Iowa State University (U.S.A.) and introduced by Conard-Pyle (U.S.A.) in 1977. A cross between Prairie Princess and an unnamed seedling.

RATING: ARS 7.4.

HABIT: Up to 5 feet (1.5m). Vigorous, erect, spreading growth; hardy and disease-resistant. Leaves are smooth, olive green.

FLOWERS: Pink, double, up to 4½ inches (11cm) across. Extremely free-flowering from late spring until autumn frosts. Fragrant.

USES: Hedging; lining driveways. Sensational massed in beds and borders.

CATHEDRAL

TYPE: Floribunda

ORIGIN: Hybridized and introduced by the House of McGredy (New Zealand) in 1975. A cross between Little Darling onto Goldilocks and Irish Mist.

RATING: ARS 7.4. All-America Award 1976; Gold Medal New Zealand 1976.

HABIT: Up to 4 feet (1.2m). Erect, bushy, branching growth; resistant to mildew disease. Leaves are semiglossy, light to dark green.

FLOWERS: Apricot with salmon shades, double, up to 5 inches (13cm) across, borne in clusters. Slightly fragrant.

USES: Effective massed in beds and borders. Superb cut flower; exhibition quality.

CHAMPAGNE

TYPE: Hybrid tea

ORIGIN: Hybridized by Robert V. Lindquist (U.S.A.) and introduced by Howard Rose Company (U.S.A.) in 1961. A cross between Charlotte Armstrong and Duquesa de Penaranda.

RATING: ARS 6.9.

HABIT: 4 feet (1.2m). Upright, bushy growth. Leaves are leathery, dark green.

FLOWERS: Buff-white shading to apricot at the petal center, double, large, up to 5 inches (13cm) across. High-centered in the mature bud stage. Delightfully fragrant.

USES: Mixed beds and borders. Cherished by flower arrangers.

CHAMPLAIN

TYPE: Shrub rose

ORIGIN: Hybridized by Felicitas Svejda (Canada) and introduced by Agriculture Canada in 1982. A cross between *R. Kordesii* and an unnamed seedling onto a cross between Red Dawn and Suzanne.

RATING: Not rated by the American Rose Society.

HABIT: 4 feet (1.2m). Dense, bushy growth; hardy. Prickly canes bear small, yellowish green leaves.

FLOWERS: Dark red, double, up to 3 inches (7.5cm) across, borne in clusters. Slightly fragrant.

USES: Mostly used as a background or hedge.

CHAMPNEY'S PINK CLUSTER

TYPE: Old garden rose

ORIGIN: Hybridized by Champney (France) in 1811. A cross between *R. chinensis* and *R. moschata*. The first rose classified as a Noisette, sometimes called Champney's Rose.

RATING: Not rated by the American Rose Society.

HABIT: Up to 6 feet (1.8m). Vigorous, low, bushy growth; moderately hardy. Arching canes bear small, semiglossy, medium green leaves.

FLOWERS: Pink, double, up to 2 inches (4cm) across, borne in large clusters. Recurrent bloom, especially in the autumn. Lightly fragrant.

USES: Attractive accent for perennial gardens. Mostly seen in old rose collections.

CHARISMA

TYPE: Floribunda

ORIGIN: Hybridized by E. G. Hill Co. (U.S.A.) and introduced by Conrad-Pyle (U.S.A.) in 1977. A cross between Gemini and Zorina.

RATING: ARS 7.2.

HABIT: 4 feet (1.2m). Upright, bushy growth. Leaves are glossy, leathery, dark green.

FLOWERS: Scarlet-and-yellow bicolor, fully double with 40 petals, up to 2½ inches (6.5cm) across, borne in clusters. High-centered in the mature bud stage. Slightly fragrant.

USES: Mixed beds and borders. Good for cutting.

CHARLES DE MILLS

TYPE: Old garden rose

ORIGIN: Believed to be a Gallica introduced in the 1800s.

RATING: ARS 8.5.

HABIT: Up to 5 feet (1.5m). Vigorous, erect, bushy growth; hardy and disease-resistant. Almost thorn-free canes bear medium green leaves.

FLOWERS: Deep magenta, fully double, like a pom-pom; up to 4½ inches (11cm) across. Bloooms once in early summer. Fragrant.

USES: Accent in old-fashioned cottage-style gardens.

CHARLOTTE ARMSTRONG

TYPE: Hybrid tea

ORIGIN: Hybridized by Dr. W. E. Lammerts (U.S.A.) in 1940 and introduced by Armstrong Roses (U.S.A.) in 1940. A cross between Soeur Therese and Crimson Glory.

RATING: ARS 7.2. All-America Award 1941; American Rose Society John Cook Medal 1941; American Rose Society David Fuerstenberg Prize 1941; Gold Medal Portland 1941; American Rose Society Gertrude M. Hubbard Gold Medal 1945; Royal National Rose Society Gold Medal 1950.

HABIT: Up to 5 feet (1.5m). Vigorous, upright growth; hardy and disease-resistant. Leaves are leathery, dark green.

FLOWERS: Blood-red in bud opening to deep pink, up to 4½ inches (11cm) across. Repeat blooming. Fragrant.

USES: Massing in beds and borders.

CHERISH

TYPE: Floribunda

ORIGIN: Hybridized by William Warriner (U.S.A.) and introduced by Jackson & Perkins (U.S.A.) in 1980. Resulting from a cross between Bridal Pink and Matador.

RATING: ARS 7.8. All-America Rose Selection 1980.

HABIT: 4 feet (1.2m). Compact, spreading growth. Leaves are attractive, dark green.

FLOWERS: Coral-pink, double, borne in clusters. Blooms are high-centered in bud stage, composed of 28 petals, and large for a floribunda (3 inches [7.5cm] across). Slightly fragrant.

USES: Massing in beds and borders. Introduced as an award-winning trio with Love (red-and-white bicolor grandiflora) and Honor (white hybrid tea).

CHEVY CHASE

TYPE: Climbing rose

ORIGIN: Developed by N. J. Hansen (England) and introduced by Bobbink & Atkins (U.S.A.) in 1939. A cross between *R. soulieana* and Eblouissant. Classified as a Rambler.

RATING: ARS 8.0. Dr. W. Van Fleet Medal 1941.

HABIT: Up to 15 feet (4.6m). Vigorous, long, arching growth; hardy and disease-resistant. Leaves are wrinkled, light green.

FLOWERS: Crimson, double, buttonlike blooms, up to 1½ inches (4cm) across, borne in dense clusters in late spring. Fragrant.

USES: Can be trained to climb up trellis and arbors. When planted on top of terraces, the heavy flowering canes cascade in an avalanche of beautiful blossoms.

CHICAGO PEACE

TYPE: Hybrid tea

ORIGIN: Discovered by Johnston (U.S.A.) and introduced by Conard-Pyle (U.S.A.) and Universal Rose Selections (France) in 1962. A sport of Peace, discovered in the rose garden at Cantigny Museum, near Chicago.

RATING: ARS 8.3. Gold Medal Portland 1961.

HABIT: Up to 5 feet (1.5m). Vigorous, upright growth; hardy. Leaves are large, glossy, dark green.

FLOWERS: Deep yellow with deep pink petal edges, high-centered up to 5½ inches (14cm) across. Repeat blooming. Slight fragrance.

USES: Mostly used for bedding. A better color combination than the original Peace rose.

CHRISTIAN DIOR

TYPE: Hybrid tea

ORIGIN: Hybridized by the House of Meilland (France) in 1958 and introduced by Universal Rose Selections (France) in 1958, Conrad-Pyle (U.S.A.) in 1961. A cross between a seedling of Independence and Happiness onto a seedling of Peace and Happiness.

RATING: ARS 7.7. All-America Award 1962; Gold Medal Geneva 1958. One of North America's top-selling roses.

HABIT: Up to 5 feet (1.5m). Vigorous, upright, branching growth; dark green glossy leaves. Slightly fragrant.

FLOWERS: Rich red, double, up to 4½ inches (11cm) across. Slightly fragrant.

USES: Effective for bedding. Long-lasting as a cut flower.

CHRYSLER IMPERIAL

TYPE: Hybrid tea

ORIGIN: Hybridized by Dr. W. E. Lammerts (U.S.A.) in 1952 and introduced by Germain's Roses (U.S.A.) in 1952. A cross between Charlotte Armstrong and Mirandy.

RATING: ARS 8.3. All-America Award 1953; Gold Medal Portland 1951; American Rose Society John Cook Medal 1964; James Alexander Gamble Rose Fragrance Medal 1965.

HABIT: Up to 5 feet (1.5m). Vigorous, upright, bushy growth. Winter-hardy canes are susceptible to mildew. Leaves are semiglossy, dark green.

FLOWERS: Dark red, double, up to 5 inches (13cm) across. Repeat flowering. Heavy clovelike fragrance.

USES: Colorful bedding rose, good exhibition-quality flower form.

CIRCUS

TYPE: Floribunda

ORIGIN: Hybridized and introduced by Armstrong Roses (U.S.A.) in 1956. A cross between Fandango and Pinocchio.

RATING: ARS 7.0. Gold Medals, Geneva 1956, Royal National Rose Society 1955; All-America Selection 1956.

HABIT: 4 feet (1.2m). Bushy growth. Leaves are leathery, dark green.

FLOWERS: Yellow flushed with pink, salmon, and scarlet. Double blooms, up to 2 inches (5cm) across, form in large clusters. Fragrant.

USES: Beds and borders. The climbing form is best trained along a fence or wall.

CITY OF YORK

TYPE: Climbing rose

ORIGIN: Hybridized by the House of Tantau (Germany) and introduced by Conard-Pyle (U.S.A.) in 1945. A cross between Professor Gnau and Dorothy Perkins.

RATING: Not rated by the American Rose Society. Gold Medal American Rose Society 1950.

HABIT: Up to 20 feet (6m) tall. Vigorous, upright growth; good winter hardiness and disease-free. Thorny canes bear glossy, dark green leaves.

FLOWERS: White, semidouble, up to 3½ inches (9cm) across. Very heavy bloom production. Fragrant.

USES: Especially good trained along the top of walls. Also suitable for covering arbors.

COLOR MAGIC

TYPE: Hybrid tea

ORIGIN: Hybridized by William Warriner (U.S.A.) and introduced by Jackson & Perkins (U.S.A.) in 1978. A cross between Spellbinder and an unnamed seedling.

RATING: ARS 8.0. All-America Award 1978.

HABIT: Up to 4 feet (1.2m). Upright, branching growth; disease-resistant, but plants need protection in severe winters. Leaves are large, glossy, dark green.

FLOWERS: White with deep pink petal tips, double, high-centered, up to 5 inches (13cm) across. Slightly fragrant.

USES: Massed bedding. Good cut flower and show rose.

COMMAND PERFORMANCE

TYPE: Hybrid tea

ORIGIN: Hybridized by Robert V. Lindquist (U.S.A.) and introduced by the Howard Rose Company (U.S.A.) in 1970. A cross between Tropicana and Hawaii.

RATING: ARS 7.2. All-America Award 1971.

HABIT: Up to 6 feet (1.8m). Upright, slender growth. Leaves are large, leathery, dark green, susceptible to mildew.

FLOWERS: Orange-red, double, high-centered, up to 4 inches (10cm) across. Continuous flowering. Fragrant.

USES: Bedding. Good for cutting.

COMTE DE CHAMBORD

TYPE: Old garden rose

ORIGIN: Introduced by Robert & Moreau (France) in 1860. Generally classified as a Portland rose, a class which resembles Bourbon roses but with repeat flowering potential during cool weather.

RATING: ARS 7.0.

HABIT: Up to 4 feet (1.2m). Erect, bushy, arching growth; hardy and disease-resistant. Thorny canes bear glossy, medium green leaves. Needs rigorous thinning every winter.

FLOWERS: Light pink deepening to rose-pink toward the petal base; double, flat, up to 3 inches (7.5cm) across. Continuous flowering during cool weather if dead-headed. Highly fragrant.

USES: Accent in cottage-style gardens, especially in mixed perennial borders.

CONDESA DE SANTAGO

TYPE: Hybrid tea

ORIGIN: Hybridized by Pedro Dot (Spain) and introduced by Conard-Pyle (U.S.A.) in 1932. Resulting from a cross between Souvenir de Claudius Pernet and Marechal Foch with Margaret McGredy.

RATING: Not rated by the American Rose Society. Gold Medal Rome 1933.

HABIT: Up to 6 feet (1.8m). Vigorous growth, tall, often mistaken for a climber. Dark green, glossy leaves.

FLOWERS: Deep pink with yellow undersides. Double with 55 petals. Cupped, up to 4 inches (10cm) across. Pleasantly fragrant.

USES: Best trained up trellis like a climbing rose.

CONFIDENCE

TYPE: Hybrid tea

ORIGIN: Hybridized by the House of Meilland (France) and introduced by Universal Rose Selections (France) in 1951 and Conard-Pyle (U.S.A.) in 1953. A cross between Peace and Michele Meilland.

RATING: ARS 8.0. Gold Medal Bagatelle (1951).

HABIT: Up to 4 feet (1.2m). Vigorous, upright, bushy growth. Leaves are leathery, dark green.

FLOWERS: Light yellow with pink petal tips, large, high-centered, up to 5 inches (13cm) across. Highly fragrant.

USES: Garden display and cutting. Similar in appearance to Peace, but a sweeter, more satisfying fragrance.

CONSTANCE SPRY

TYPE: Shrub rose

ORIGIN: Developed by David Austin (Great Britain) in 1961 and introduced by Sunningdale Nursery (Great Britain). A cross between Belle Isle and Dainty Maid.

RATING: Not rated by the American Rose Society.

HABIT: 6 to 10 feet (1.8 to 3m). Upright, bushy, arching growth; hardy and disease-resistant. Thorny canes bear glossy, dark green leaves.

FLOWERS: Pink, double, up to 5 inches (13cm) across, with a swirling old-fashioned garden rose form. Myrrhlike fragrance.

USES: Accent in mixed beds and borders; training along fences. Popular with floral arrangers.

CRESTED MOSS (CHAPEAU DE NAPOLEON)

TYPE: Old garden rose

ORIGIN: A variety of *Rosa centifolia*, discovered growing on the wall of a ruined Swiss convent and introduced in 1827. Classified as a Moss rose.

RATING: ARS 8.7.

HABIT: Up to 5 feet (1.5m). Erect, shrubby, arching growth; hardy and disease-resistant. Leaves are medium size, dark green.

FLOWERS: Deep pink, double, up to 4 inches (10cm) across. Moderately fragrant.

USES: Good accent for old stone walls, low fences, and informal cottage-style gardens.

CRIMSON GLORY

TYPE: Hybrid tea

ORIGIN: Hybridized by the House of Kordes (Germany) and introduced by Dreer (U.S.A.) and Jackson & Perkins (U.S.A.) in 1935. A cross between a Catherine Kordes seedling and W. E. Chaplin.

RATING: ARS 7.2. Gold Medal National Rose Society 1936; James Alexander Gamble Rose Fragrance Medal 1961.

HABIT: Up to 4 feet (1.2m). Vigorous, bushy, spreading growth; hardy and disease-resistant. Leaves are leathery, dark green, glossy.

FLOWERS: Crimson-red, double, up to 4½ inches (11cm) across. Very fragrant, velvety texture.

USES: Good garden display. One plant makes a colorful free-flowering accent.

DAINTY BESS

TYPE: Hybrid tea

ORIGIN: Introduced by Archer (Great Britain) in 1925. Resulting from a cross between Ophelia and King of Kings.

RATING: ARS 8.8. Gold Medal Royal National Rose Society 1935.

HABIT: 4 feet (1.2m); a climbing form reaches 10 feet (3m). Vigorous, upright growth. Leaves are leathery, dark green.

FLOWERS: Rose-pink, single, with maroon stamens, 5 petals. Individual flowers up to 5 inches (13cm) across. Fragrant.

USES: Mixed beds and borders. Climbing form suitable for covering trellis and arbors.

DIAMOND JUBILEE

TYPE: Hybrid tea

ORIGIN: Hybridized by Eugene Boerner (U.S.A.) and introduced by Jackson & Perkins (U.S.A.) in 1947. Resulting from a cross between Marechal Niel and Feu Pernet-Ducher.

RATING: ARS 6.5. All-America Selection 1948.

HABIT: 3 to 4 feet (.9 to 1.2m). Upright, compact growth. Leaves are leathery, dark green.

FLOWERS: Buff-yellow, large, double with 28 petals, up to 6 inches (15cm) across. Opens out into a cup shape. Slightly fragrant.

USES: Mixed beds and borders. Good for cutting.

DOLLY PARTON

TYPE: Hybrid tea

ORIGIN: Hybridized by Joseph Winchel (U.S.A.) and introduced by Conard-Pyle (U.S.A.) in 1984. A cross between Fragrant Cloud and Oklahoma.

RATING: ARS 7.4. American Rose Center Trial Garden Bronze Certificate.

HABIT: Up to 5 feet (1.5m). Vigorous, erect growth. Thick canes bear medium-size, semiglossy, dark green leaves.

FLOWERS: Deep orange-red, very large, double, up to 6 inches (15cm) across. Highly fragrant.

USES: Garden display. One plant can make a colorful accent. Sensational cut flower.

DON JUAN

TYPE: Climbing rose

ORIGIN: Hybridized by Michelle Malandrone (Italy) and introduced by Jackson & Perkins (U.S.A.) in 1958. A cross between a seedling of New Dawn and New Yorker.

RATING: ARS 8.3.

HABIT: Up to 8 feet (2.4m). Vigorous, tall growth; hardy and disease-resistant. Leaves are large, glossy, dark green.

FLOWERS: Dark red, double, up to 5 inches (13cm) across. Fragrant, with a velvety texture.

USES: Training up trellis, over fences and arbors. Larger-flowered and more fragrant than Blaze.

DORTMUND

TYPE: Shrub rose

ORIGIN: Hybridized by the House of Kordes (Germany) and introduced in 1955. A cross between *R. kordesii* and an unnamed seedling. Classified as Kordesii.

RATING: ARS 9.1 (the highest-rated shrub rose).

HABIT: Up to 12 feet (3.7m). Vigorous growth; winter-hardy, disease-free. Leaves are glossy, dark green.

FLOWERS: Red with white eye, single, up to 3½ inches (9cm) across, saucer-shaped, borne in large clusters. Blooms heavily in spring, with some repeat bloom followed by decorative red hips in autumn. Lightly fragrant.

USES: Excellent for training along walls, trellis, over arbors.

DOUBLE DELIGHT

TYPE: Hybrid tea

ORIGIN: Hybridized and introduced by Armstrong Roses (U.S.A.) in 1977. A cross between Granada and Garden Party.

RATING: ARS 8.8. All-America Award 1977; Gold Medals, Rome 1976, Baden-Baden 1976; James Alexander Gamble Rose Fragrance Medal 1986.

HABIT: Up to 4 feet (1.2m). Vigorous, upright, bushy growth; needs protection in severe winters; susceptible to mildew. Leaves are dull, dark green.

FLOWERS: Creamy white inner petals and strawberry red outer petals, fully double, up to 5½ inches (14cm) across. Highly fragrant.

USES: Good garden display. Excellent for cutting.

DR. HUEY

TYPE: Climbing rose

ORIGIN: Hybridized by Captain Thomas (U.S.A.) in 1914 and introduced by Bobbink & Atkins (U.S.A.) in 1920 and A. N. Pierson (U.S.A.) in 1920. A cross between Ethel and Grüss an Teplitz.

RATING: Not rated by the American Rose Society. American Rose Society Gertrude M. Hubbard Gold Medal 1924.

HABIT: 12 to 18 feet (3.7 to 5.5m). Vigorous growth; hardy and disease-resistant. Tall, upright. Thorny canes bear medium-size, glossy, dark green leaves.

FLOWERS: Dark red, semidouble, 3½ inches (9cm) across. Blooms cover the canes in dense clusters in spring. Fragrant.

USES: Training over arches, gazebos, up strong trellis to cover walls and fences.

DR. W. VAN FLEET

TYPE: Climbing rose

ORIGIN: Hybridized by Van Fleet (U.S.A.) and introduced by Peter Henderson Co. (U.S.A.) in 1910. A cross between *R. wichuraiana* and Safrano onto Souvenir du President Carnot.

RATING: ARS 7.5.

HABIT: Up to 20 feet (6m). Vigorous growth; tall, disease-resistant. Leaves are glossy, dark green.

FLOWERS: Light pink fading to white, double, up to 3 inches (7.5cm) across. Spring-blooming. Fragrant.

USES: Best when trained along fencing and pruned in winter to encourage bushy growth. New Dawn is a sport of Dr. W. Van Fleet with recurrent flowering.

DUCHESS

TYPE: Hybrid tea

ORIGIN: Hybridized by J. Van Veen (Holland) and introduced by Carlton Rose Nursery (U.S.A.) in 1976. Resulting from a cross between White Satin and an unnamed seedling.

RATING: Not rated by the American Rose Society.

HABIT: 4 feet (1.2m). Upright, bushy growth. Leaves are leathery, glossy, dark green.

FLOWERS: Cameo pink with deeper shading, large, double, high-centered, up to 4½ inches (11cm) across. Fragrant.

USES: Garden display in beds and borders. Also suitable for cutting.

ECLIPSE

TYPE: Hybrid tea

ORIGIN: Hybridized by J. H. Nicolas (U.S.A.) and introduced by Jackson & Perkins (U.S.A.) in 1935. Resulting from a cross between Joanna Hill and Federico Casas.

RATING: ARS 5.7. Gold Medals, Portland 1935, Rome 1935, Bagatelle 1936; American Rose Society David Fuerstenberg Prize 1938.

HABIT: 5 feet (1.5m). Vigorous, upright, bushy growth. Leaves are leathery, dark green.

FLOWERS: Deep golden yellow in bud, opening out to bright yellow, loose, 4½-inch (11.5cm) double blooms with 28 petals. Fragrant.

USES: Since the mature bud is remarkably long and pointed, it is valued as a cut flower.

EL CAPITAN

TYPE: Grandiflora

ORIGIN: Hybridized and introduced by Armstrong Roses (U.S.A.) in 1959. Resulting from a cross between Charlotte Armstrong and Floradora.

RATING: ARS 7.8. Gold Medal Portland 1959.

HABIT: 5 feet (1.5m). Vigorous, upright, bushy growth. Leaves are glossy, dark green.

FLOWERS: Cherry red, double with 30 petals, up to 5 inches (13cm) across, held in small clusters. High-centered in the mature bud stage. Especially large when grown in a cool coastal climate. Slightly fragrant.

USES: Garden display, though may need staking.

ELECTRON

TYPE: Hybrid tea

ORIGIN: Hybridized and introduced by the House of McGredy (New Zealand) in 1970. A cross between Paddy McGredy and Prima Ballerina.

RATING: ARS 7.7. All-America Award 1973; Gold Medals, Great Britain 1969, The Hague 1970, Belfast 1972.

HABIT: Up to 4 feet (1.2m). Vigorous, upright, bushy growth; hardy and disease-resistant. Leaves are leathery, dark green.

FLOWERS: Rose-pink, double, high-centered, up to 5 inches (13cm) across. Fragrant.

USES: Garden display. Cutting.

ESCAPADE

TYPE: Floribunda

ORIGIN: Hybridized and introduced by R. Harkness Rose Gardens (England) in 1967. Resulting from a cross between Pink Parfait and Baby Faurax.

RATING: ARS 8.2. Gold Medals, Baden-Baden 1969, Belfast 1969.

HABIT: 4 feet (1.2m). Vigorous, bushy growth. Leaves are glossy, light green.

FLOWERS: Magenta-red with white centers surrounding a golden crown of stamens; semidouble, 12-petaled, up to 3 inches (7.5cm) across, borne in dense clusters. Fragrant.

USES: Good for massing in borders and cascading over walls and fences.

EUROPEANA

TYPE: Floribunda

ORIGIN: Hybridized by George De Reuter (Holland) in 1963 and introduced by Conard-Pyle (U.S.A.) in 1968. A cross between Ruth Leuwerik and Rosemary Rose.

RATING: ARS 9.0. All-America Award 1968; Gold Medal The Hague 1962.

HABIT: Up to 3 feet (.9m). Upright, compact, branching growth; hardy and disease-resistant. Leaves turn from red to glossy, dark green.

FLOWERS: Crimson-red, double, up to 3 inches (7.5cm) across, borne in dense clusters. Extremely free-flowering from late spring until autumn frosts. Little fragrance.

USES: Excellent for massed bedding and cutting.

EYEPAINT

TYPE: Floribunda

ORIGIN: Introduced by the House of McGredy (New Zealand) in 1975. A cross between an unnamed seedling onto Picasso.

RATING: ARS 8.0. Gold Medals, Belfast 1978, Baden-Baden 1974.

HABIT: Up to 4 feet (1.2m). Vigorous, upright, spreading growth; hardy, but highly susceptible to black spot. Thorny canes bear small, dark green leaves.

FLOWERS: Magenta-red with white eye and golden crown of stamens; single, up to 2½ inches (6.5cm) across, borne in wide, flat clusters. Slightly fragrant.

USES: Best used in borders along walls, fences, and especially terraces where the top-heavy arching canes can cascade.

FANTIN-LATOUR

TYPE: Old garden rose

ORIGIN: Hybridizer unknown. Named for the famous nineteenth-century French Impressionist painter. Classified as a Centifolia hybrid.

RATING: ARS 7.6.

HABIT: Up to 6 feet (1.8m). Erect, spreading growth; hardy and disease-resistant. Leaves are semiglossy, medium green.

FLOWERS: Pale pink with a button eye, double, flat, up to 3½ inches (9cm) across. Highly fragrant.

USES: Accent in cottage-style gardens. Popular ingredient in potpourri. Blooms mostly in early summer in cool weather.

FASHION

TYPE: Floribunda

ORIGIN: Hybridized by Eugene Boerner (U.S.A.) and introduced by Jackson & Perkins (U.S.A.) in 1949. A cross between Pinocchio and Crimson Glory.

RATING: ARS 7.7. All-America Award 1950; Gold Medals, National Rose Society 1948, Bagatelle 1949, Portland 1949, American Rose Society 1954; American Rose Society David Fuerstenberg Prize 1950.

HABIT: Up to 4 feet (1.2m). Vigorous, bushy, spreading growth; hardy and disease-resistant. Leaves are semiglossy, medium green.

FLOWERS: Coral-pink, double, up to 3½ inches (9cm) across, borne in clusters of four to six flowers. Continuous blooming. Slight fragrance.

USES: Formal bedding displays and informal garden accents, especially against stone walls and fences.

FIRE KING

TYPE: Floribunda

ORIGIN: Hybridized by the House of Meilland (France) and introduced by Universal Rose Selections (France) in 1958 and Conard-Pyle (U.S.A.) in 1959. A cross between Moulin Rouge and Fashion.

RATING: ARS 7.5. All-America Award 1960.

HABIT: Up to 4 feet (1.2m). Vigorous, upright, bushy growth. Leaves are leathery, green.

FLOWERS: Scarlet-red, double, camellia-shaped, up to 3 inches (7.5cm) across, borne in dense clusters. Musklike fragrance.

USES: Massed bedding; good accent in mixed borders. One stem creates an instant bouquet for cut flower arrangements.

FIRECRACKER

TYPE: Floribunda

ORIGIN: Hybridized by Eugene Boerner (U.S.A.) and introduced by Jackson & Perkins (U.S.A.) in 1959. Resulting from a cross between a seedling of Pinocchio and a seedling of Numa Fay.

RATING: Not rated by the American Rose Society.

HABIT: 3 feet (.9m). Bushy, compact, spreading growth. Leaves are leathery, light green.

FLOWERS: Flaming scarlet lightening to yellow at the petal base, semidouble, up to 4½ inches (11cm) across, borne in clusters. Unusually large for a floribunda. Fragrant.

USES: Massing in beds and borders.

FIRST EDITION

TYPE: Floribunda

ORIGIN: Hybridized by the House of Delbard (France) and introduced by Conard-Pyle (U.S.A.) in 1976. A complex cross involving Zambra, Orleans, and Goldilocks onto an Orange Triumph seedling and Floradora.

RATING: ARS 8.4. All-America Award 1977.

HABIT: Up to 4 feet (1.2m). Vigorous, erect, bushy growth; disease-resistant but needs protection in severe winters. Leaves are large, glossy, olive green.

FLOWERS: Coral with an orange highlight at the petal center, double, up to 3 inches (7.5cm) across. Borne in tight clusters. Continuous flowering, slightly fragrant.

USES: Massing in beds; effective grown in containers.

FIRST PRIZE

TYPE: Hybrid tea

ORIGIN: Hybridized by Eugene Boerner (U.S.A.) and introduced by Jackson & Perkins (U.S.A.) in 1970. Resulting from a cross between a seedling of Enchantment and a seedling of Golden Masterpiece.

RATING: ARS 8.9. All-America Rose Selection 1970; American Rose Society Gertrude M. Hubbard Gold Medal 1971.

HABIT: 4 feet (1.2m); climbing First Prize reaches 8 feet (2.4m). Vigorous, upright growth. Leaves are leathery, dark green.

FLOWERS: Rose-pink blending to ivory-white, double, up to 5 inches (13cm) across, high-centered. Fragrant.

USES: Beds and borders. Exquisite cut flower.

F. J. GROOTENDORST

TYPE: Shrub rose

ORIGIN: Developed by de Goey (Holland) and introduced by F. J. Grootendorst (Holland) in 1918. A cross between *R. rugosa rubra* and an unknown Polyantha rose. Classified as a hybrid Rugosa.

RATING: ARS 8.0.

HABIT: Up to 8 feet (2.4m). Upright, bushy growth; hardy and disease-resistant. Thorny canes bear small, textured, dark green leaves.

FLOWERS: Scarlet-red (though there are several other color sports), double, 1½ inches (4cm) across, borne abundantly in dense clusters. Repeat blooming. No fragrance.

USES: Popular accent in old-fashioned cottage-style gardens and herb gardens. Combines well with perennials.

FORTY-NINER

TYPE: Hybrid tea

ORIGIN: Hybridized and introduced by Armstrong Roses (U.S.A.) in 1949. A cross between Contrast and Charlotte Armstrong.

RATING: ARS 5.8. All-America Rose Selection 1949; Gold Medal Portland 1947.

HABIT: 4 feet (1.2m). Vigorous, upright growth. Leaves are leathery, glossy, dark green.

FLOWERS: Red with yellow reverse; large, double with 33 petals, up to 4 inches (10cm) across. Slightly fragrant.

USES: Beds and borders. Mature buds are long and pointed, exquisite for cutting.

FRAGRANT CLOUD

TYPE: Hybrid tea

ORIGIN: Hybridized by the House of Tantau (Germany) in 1963 and introduced by Jackson & Perkins (U.S.A.) in 1963. A cross between Prima Ballerina and an unnamed seedling.

RATING: ARS 8.0. Gold Medal National Rose Society 1963; Gold Medal Portland 1967; James Alexander Gamble Rose Fragrance Medal 1969.

HABIT: Up to 5 feet (1.5m). Upright, branching growth; hardy and disease-resistant. Leaves are glossy, dark green.

FLOWERS: Coral-red, double, up to 5 inches (13cm) across; often borne in pairs. Powerful, pleasant aroma.

USES: Garden display, cutting. Just one bloom in a vase will fill a room with fragrance.

FRAGRANT HOUR

TYPE: Hybrid tea

ORIGIN: Hybridized by the House of McGredy (New Zealand) and introduced in 1973. Resulting from a cross between Arthur Bell and Spartan crossed with Grand Gala.

RATING: ARS 7.0. Gold Medal Belfast 1975.

HABIT: 4 feet (1.2m). Upright, bushy growth. Leaves are light green.

FLOWERS: Bronze-pink, double with 35 petals, high-pointed, up to 4½ inches (11cm) across. Extremely fragrant.

USES: Beds and borders. The extra-large blooms are heavy, and stems may need staking to keep erect.

FRAU DAGMAR HARTOPP (FRAU DAGMAR HASTRUP)

TYPE: Shrub rose

ORIGIN: Unknown German origin, introduced about 1914. Parentage unknown. Classified as a hybrid Rugosa.

RATING: ARS 8.7.

HABIT: Up to 4 feet (1.2m). Dense, spreading growth; hardy and disease-resistant. Thorny canes bear glossy, dark green leaves.

FLOWERS: Light pink, single, up to 3½ inches (9cm) across. Continuous flowering. Clove-scented. Conspicuous golden stamens and decorative bright red hips in autumn.

USES: Good accent for mixed borders and old-fashioned, cottage-style gardens.

FRENCH LACE

TYPE: Floribunda

ORIGIN: Hybridized by William Warriner (U.S.A.) and introduced by Jackson & Perkins (U.S.A.) in 1981. A cross between Dr. A. J. Verhage and Bridal Pink.

RATING: ARS 7.8. All-America Award 1982.

HABIT: Up to 4 feet (1.2m). Erect, bushy, branching growth; disease-resistant and hardy. Leaves are glossy, dark green.

FLOWERS: Ivory-white flushed with peach, double, high-centered, borne in small clusters. Individual flowers measure up to 4 inches (10cm) across. Blooms resemble hybrid teas. Slightly fragrant.

USES: Exhibition-quality blooms are prized by flower arrangers, especially in the mature bud stage. Worth growing in pots where space is limited on account of its good repeat bloom.

FRIENDSHIP

TYPE: Hybrid tea

ORIGIN: Hybridized by Robert V. Lindquist (U.S.A.) and introduced by Conard-Pyle (U.S.A.) in 1978. A cross between Fragrant Cloud and Miss All-American Beauty.

RATING: ARS 7.0. All-America Rose Selection 1979.

HABIT: 4 to 5 feet (1.2 to 1.5m). Vigorous, upright growth. Leaves are large, dark green.

FLOWERS: Deep pink, double, with 28 petals opening out into a cup-shaped bloom that is unusually large, up to 6 inches (15cm) across. Very fragrant.

USES: Beds and borders. The heavy flower stems may need staking.

FRUHLINGSGOLD (SPRING GOLD)

TYPE: Old garden rose

ORIGIN: Hybridized by the House of Kordes (Germany) in 1937 and introduced by Bobbink & Atkins (U.S.A.) in 1951. A cross between Joanna Hill and *Rosa spinosissima hispida*. Classified as a hybrid Spinosissima.

RATING: Not rated by the American Rose Society.

HABIT: 4 feet (1.2m). Very vigorous, bushy, spreading growth. Extremely thorny canes bear large, heavily textured, light green leaves.

FLOWERS: Orange pointed buds open out to creamy yellow, single blooms up to 3 inches (7.5cm) across. Have 5 to 10 petals. Highly fragrant.

USES: Informal hedging, ground cover.

GARDEN PARTY

TYPE: Hybrid tea

ORIGIN: Hybridized and introduced by Armstrong Roses (U.S.A.) in 1959. A cross between Charlotte Armstrong and Peace.

RATING: ARS 8.5. All-America Award 1960; Gold Medal Bagatelle 1959.

HABIT: Up to 4 feet (1.2m). Vigorous, upright, branching growth. Leaves are large, lustrous, dark green.

FLOWERS: Cream center with a blush of pink at the petal tips, up to 5 inches (13cm) across. Fragrant.

USES: Garden display; exhibition quality. Good for cutting.

GENE BOERNER

TYPE: Floribunda

ORIGIN: Hybridized by Eugene Boerner (U.S.A.) and introduced by Jackson & Perkins (U.S.A.) in 1968. A cross between Ginger and Ma Perkins onto Garnette Supreme.

RATING: ARS 8.7. All-America Award 1969.

HABIT: Up to 5 feet (1.5m). Vigorous growth; hardy and disease-resistant. Thorny, branching canes bear semiglossy, medium green leaves.

FLOWERS: Pink, double, resembling miniature hybrid teas, but borne in tight clusters. Individual flowers measure up to 3 inches (7.5cm) across. Slightly fragrant.

USES: Good accent in mixed borders. Excellent for cutting.

GEORGIA

TYPE: Hybrid tea

ORIGIN: Hybridized and introduced by the House of Weeks (U.S.A.) in 1980. Resulting from a cross between Arizona and an unnamed seedling.

RATING: ARS 6.3.

HABIT: 5 feet (1.5m). Tall growth. Sharp-thorned canes bear large, leathery, dark green leaves.

FLOWERS: Peach-apricot blend, double with 53 petals, up to 4½ inches (11.5cm) across. Moderately scented.

USES: Beds and borders. Excellent for cutting.

GOLDBUSCH

TYPE: Shrub rose

ORIGIN: Hybridized by the House of Kordes (Germany) and introduced in 1954.

RATING: ARS 7.1.

HABIT: 4 to 5 feet (1.2 to 1.5m). Vigorous, upright, bushy growth. Leaves are leathery, glossy, light green.

FLOWERS: Yellow, semidouble, borne in large clusters of up to 20 blooms. Individual flowers measure up to 3 inches (7.5cm) across. Fragrant.

USES: Good highlight for mixed perennial borders; suitable for hedging.

GOLD COIN

TYPE: Miniature

ORIGIN: Hybridized by R. S. Moore (U.S.A.) and introduced by Sequoia Nurseries (U.S.A.) in 1967. A cross between Golden Glow and Magic Wand.

RATING: ARS 7.5.

HABIT: Up to 12 inches (31cm). Dwarf, compact growth. Leaves are leathery, dark green.

FLOWERS: Golden yellow, double, tea rose shape, up to 1½ inches (4cm) across. Light fragrance.

USES: Edging beds and borders, pots, hanging baskets, house plant.

GOLDEN SHOWERS

TYPE: Climbing rose

ORIGIN: Hybridized by Dr. W. E. Lammerts (U.S.A.) and introduced by Germain's Roses (U.S.A.) in 1956. A cross between Charlotte Armstrong and Captain Thomas.

RATING: ARS 6.9. All-America Award 1957; Gold Medal Portland 1960.

HABIT: Up to 12 feet (3.7m) tall. Vigorous, rambling growth; hardy and disease-resistant. Almost thorn-free canes bear leathery, glossy, dark green leaves.

FLOWERS: Golden yellow, fully double, up to 4 inches (10cm) across—unusually large for a climber. Moderately fragrant.

USES: Sensational trained up old walls, old ironwork, and barn siding. Suitable for covering fences, arbors, and trellis.

GOLDEN WINGS

TYPE: Shrub rose

ORIGIN: Developed by David A. V. Shepherd (Great Britain) and introduced by Bosley Nursery (Great Britain) in 1956. From a cross between Soeur Therese onto a seedling of *Rosa spinosissima altaica* and Ormiston Roy.

RATING: ARS 8.5. National Gold Medal Certificate 1958.

HABIT: Up to 6 feet (1.8m). Vigorous, upright, bushy growth; hardy and disease-resistant. Thorny canes bear light green leaves.

FLOWERS: Sulphur-yellow, single, up to 5 inches (13cm) across. Recurrent blooming from spring through autumn. Slightly fragrant.

USES: Good accent in mixed beds and borders, especially combined with perennials.

GOLD MEDAL

TYPE: Grandiflora

ORIGIN: Hybridized and introduced by Armstrong Roses (U.S.A.) in 1982. A cross between Yellow Pages with Granada and Garden Party.

RATING: ARS 8.0.

HABIT: 4 feet (1.2m). Upright, bushy growth. Leaves are large, dark green.

FLOWERS: Deep golden yellow sometimes tinged with apricot. Double with 38 petals, long and pointed in the mature bud stage, open out to 5 inches (13cm) across. Slightly fragrant.

USES: Beds and borders. Exquisite cut flower.

GRAHAM THOMAS

TYPE: Shrub rose

ORIGIN: Hybridized and introduced by David Austin (Great Britain) in 1983. A cross between an unnamed seedling and Charles Austin onto an Iceberg seedling.

RATING: Not rated by the American Rose Society.

HABIT: Up to 5 feet (1.5m). Upright, bushy, arching growth. Leaves are small, glossy, dark green.

FLOWERS: Rich, deep yellow, fully double, up to 4 inches (10cm) across, cupped like old-fashioned shrub roses. Recurrent blooming. Highly fragrant.

USES: Good accent for mixed beds and borders. Suitable for informal hedges. Probably the most popular of a series of new roses known as English old rose hybrids.

GRANADA

TYPE: Hybrid tea

ORIGIN: Hybridized by Robert V. Lindquist (U.S.A.) and introduced by the Howard Rose Company (U.S.A.) in 1963. A cross between Tiffany and Cavalcade.

RATING: ARS 8.4. All-America Award 1964; James Alexander Gamble Rose Fragrance Medal 1968.

HABIT: Up to 6 feet (1.8m). Vigorous, upright, branching growth; needs protection during severe winters. Thorny canes bear leathery, dark green leaves.

FLOWERS: Blend of rose-pink, nasturtium-red, and lemon-yellow—the colors of sunset; high-centered, up to 5 inches (13cm) across. Fragrant.

USES: Popular garden rose in Mediterranean climates. Good for cutting.

GREEN ICE

TYPE: Miniature

ORIGIN: Hybridized by R. S. Moore (U.S.A.) and introduced by Sequoia Nurseries (U.S.A.) in 1971. A cross between *Rosa wichuraiana* and Floradora onto Jet Trail.

RATING: ARS 7.3.

HABIT: Up to 12 inches (31cm). Low, bushy growth. Leaves are small, leathery, glossy.

FLOWERS: White changing to light lime-green, double, up to 1½ inches (4cm) across. No fragrance.

USES: Pots, hanging baskets, dry walls, edging beds and borders.

GREEN ROSE (*R. CHINENSIS 'VIRIDIFLORA'*)

TYPE: Old garden rose

ORIGIN: Introduced from China as an oddity, and cultivated since 1845. Classified as a China rose.

RATING: Not rated by the American Rose Society.

HABIT: 3 feet (.9m). Bushy, low growth; disease-resistant but not reliably hardy. Leaves are small, dark green.

FLOWERS: Green, double, 1½ to 2 inches (4 to 5cm) across. Everblooming. No fragrance.

USES: Mostly grown as an edging to rose beds and in pots.

GYPSY

TYPE: Hybrid tea

ORIGIN: Hybridized by Swim & Weeks (U.S.A.) and introduced by Conard-Pyle (U.S.A.) in 1972. A complex cross involving Happiness onto Chrysler Imperial, crossed with El Capitan, and crossed again onto Comanche.

RATING: ARS 6.0. All-America Award 1973.

HABIT: Up to 5 feet (1.5m). Upright, vigorous, branching growth; hardy and disease-resistant. Leaves are large, glossy, dark green.

FLOWERS: Orange-red, double, high-centered, up to 4½ inches (11cm) across. Slightly fragrant.

USES: Garden display and cutting.

HANSA

TYPE: Shrub rose

ORIGIN: Introduced by Schaum & Van Tol (Holland) in 1905. Classified as hybrid Rugosa.

RATING: ARS 8.5.

HABIT: 4 to 5 feet (1.2 to 1.5m). Vigorous, bushy, spreading growth. Leaves are glossy, heavily textured, dark green.

FLOWERS: Mauve-red, double, up to 5 inches (13cm) across. Highly fragrant. Followed by large decorative red fruits.

USES: Hedging and ground cover, especially in seashore gardens to control sand movement.

HARRISON'S YELLOW

TYPE: Old garden rose

ORIGIN: Introduced in 1830 from the garden of Mr. G. F. Harrison, who lived in what is now midtown Manhattan, New York. Believed to be a natural cross between *Rosa foetida* (the Austrian Brier rose) and *Rosa spinosissima* (the Scotch rose). Classified as hybrid *foetida*.

RATING: ARS 7.6.

HABIT: Up to 7 feet (2.1m). Upright, arching growth; hardy and disease-resistant. Thorny canes bear small, light green leaves.

FLOWERS: Bright yellow, semidouble, up to 2 inches (5cm) across, studded all along the canes. Spring-blooming. Strong, yeasty fragrance.

USES: Effective when grown up a trellis against a wall and to arch over fences.

HEIRLOOM

TYPE: Hybrid tea

ORIGIN: Hybridized by William Warriner (U.S.A.) and introduced by Jackson & Perkins (U.S.A.) in 1972. A cross between unnamed seedlings.

RATING: ARS 6.5.

HABIT: 4 to 5 feet (1.2 to 1.5m). Upright growth. Leaves are leathery, dark green.

FLOWERS: Deep lilac, semidouble, up to 5 inches (13cm) across. Very fragrant.

USES: Beds and borders. Good for cutting.

HENRY HUDSON

TYPE: Shrub rose

ORIGIN: Developed by Felicitas Svejda (Canada) and introduced by the Canadian Department of Agriculture in 1976. Classified as a hybrid Rugosa.

RATING: Not rated by the American Rose Society.

HABIT: Up to 4 feet (1.2m) high. Low, bushy growth. Thorny canes bear leathery, dark green leaves.

FLOWERS: White with beautiful crown of yellow stamens at center, semidouble, up to 3 inches (7.5cm) across. Recurrent bloom. Handsome red hips. Highly fragrant.

USES: Mostly used for hedging, especially in coastal gardens because of salt tolerance.

HOLY TOLEDO

TYPE: Miniature

ORIGIN: Hybridized and introduced by Armstrong Roses (U.S.A.) in 1978. A cross between Gingersnap and Magic Carousel.

RATING: ARS 8.5. Award of Excellence American Rose Society 1980.

HABIT: Up to 20 inches (51cm). Vigorous, dwarf, bushy growth. Thorny canes bear glossy, dark green leaves.

FLOWERS: Deep orange-apricot, double, up to 2 inches (5cm) across. Slightly fragrant.

USES: Sensational pot plant, suitable for low bedding and edging; creates a beautiful tree-form rose by grafting.

HONOR

TYPE: Hybrid tea

ORIGIN: Hybridized by William Warriner (U.S.A.) and introduced by Jackson & Perkins (U.S.A.) in 1980. A cross between unknown seedlings.

RATING: ARS 7.4. All-America Rose Selection 1980, plus five international awards.

HABIT: 3 to 4 feet (.9 to 1.2m). Upright growth. Leaves are dark olive-green.

FLOWERS: White, double with 23 petals; long, pointed buds open up into loose flowers, 5 inches (13cm) wide. Slightly fragrant.

USES: Beds and borders. Introduced as an award-winning trio with Love (red-and-white bicolor grandiflora) and Cherish (coral-pink floribunda).

ICEBERG

TYPE: Floribunda

ORIGIN: Hybridized by the House of Kordes (Germany) and introduced in 1958. A cross between Robin Hood and Virgo.

RATING: ARS 8.9. Gold Medals, Royal National Rose Society 1958, Baden-Baden 1958, Great Britain 1958.

HABIT: Up to 8 feet (2.4m); climbing Iceberg grows to 12 feet (3.7m). Vigorous, upright, bushy growth; hardy, but susceptible to blackspot. Leaves are glossy, light green.

FLOWERS: Pure white, double, cup-shaped, up to 3 inches (7.5cm) across, borne in dense clusters. Fragrant.

USES: Probably the most widely planted white rose in Europe and North America. Especially popular on the west coast of North America where it produces an avalanche of flowers in spring and flowers continuously. Good component of "all-white" gardens.

IMPATIENT

TYPE: Floribunda

ORIGIN: Hybridized by William Warriner (U.S.A.) and introduced by Jackson & Perkins (U.S.A.) in 1984. A cross between America and an unnamed seedling.

RATING: ARS 8.0. All-America Award 1984.

HABIT: Up to 4 feet (1.2m). Vigorous, upright, bushy growth; disease-resistant. New foliage is red, turns dark green.

FLOWERS: Orange-red, double, up to 3 inches (7.5cm) across, borne in immense clusters. Incredibly free-flowering. Slightly fragrant.

USES: Sensational for summer bedding, especially in large masses. Impatient, Sunsprite, and Vogue make a stunning combination.

INK SPOTS

TYPE: Hybrid tea

ORIGIN: Hybridized and introduced by the House of Weeks (U.S.A.) in 1985. The result of crosses between unnamed seedlings.

RATING: ARS 6.9.

HABIT: 3 to 4 feet (.9 to 1.2m). Upright, bushy, spreading growth. Leaves are large, semiglossy, dark green.

FLOWERS: Dark red, double with 35 petals, up to 4 inches (10cm) across. Slightly fragrant.

USES: Beds and borders. Wonderful color for romantic floral arrangements.

INTRIGUE

TYPE: Floribunda

ORIGIN: Hybridized by William Warriner (U.S.A.) and introduced by Jackson & Perkins (U.S.A.) in 1984. A cross between White Masterpiece and Heirloom.

RATING: ARS 7.1. All-America Rose Selection 1984.

HABIT: 4 feet (1.2m). Upright growth. Leaves are semiglossy, dark green.

FLOWERS: Reddish purple, double with 20 petals, borne in large clusters. Individual flowers measure 3½ inches (9cm) across. Very fragrant.

USES: Beds and borders. Petals have a thick velvety substance good for potpourri.

IVORY FASHION

TYPE: Floribunda

ORIGIN: Hybridized by Eugene Boerner (U.S.A.) and introduced by Jackson & Perkins (U.S.A.) in 1958. A cross between Sonata and Fashion.

RATING: ARS 8.7. All-America Award 1959.

HABIT: Up to 4 feet (1.2m). Erect, branching growth. Almost thorn-free canes bear leathery, semiglossy, medium green leaves.

FLOWERS: Creamy white, semidouble, 4 inches (10cm) across, borne in clusters. Urn-shaped in the mature bud stage, opening out flat. Slightly fragrant.

USES: Creates an attractive low hedge. Beautiful in containers. Excellent cut flower.

JIMINI CRICKET

TYPE: Floribunda

ORIGIN: Hybridized by Eugene Boerner (U.S.A.) and introduced by Jackson & Perkins (U.S.A.) in 1954. A cross between Goldilocks and Geranium Red.

RATING: Not rated by the American Rose Society. All-America Rose Selection 1955.

HABIT: 3 to 4 feet (.9 to 1.2m). Upright, bushy growth. Leaves are glossy, medium green.

FLOWERS: Coral-pink and coral-orange, double with 28 petals, cup-shaped, to 4 inches (10cm) across, borne in clusters. Appealing spicy fragrance.

USES: Good for garden display in beds and borders, especially planted for an informal look along a wall or fence.

JOHN F. KENNEDY

TYPE: Hybrid tea

ORIGIN: Hybridized by Eugene Boerner (U.S.A.) and introduced by Jackson & Perkins (U.S.A.) in 1965. A cross between an unnamed seedling and White Queen.

RATING: ARS 6.0. A poor rating compared to other white hybrid teas, such as White Lightnin' and White Masterpiece.

HABIT: Up to 4 feet (1.2m). Erect growth; poor hardiness. Thorny canes bear medium-size, leathery, semiglossy green leaves.

FLOWERS: White, with a hint of green in the center, double, high-centered, up to 5 inches (13cm) across. Good fragrance.

USES: Garden display, mixed rose borders. Popular cut flower.

JOSEPH'S COAT

TYPE: Climbing rose

ORIGIN: Hybridized by Armstrong & Swim (U.S.A.) and introduced by Armstrong Roses (U.S.A.) in 1964. A cross between Buccaneer and Circus.

RATING: ARS 7.6. Gold Medal Bagatelle 1964.

HABIT: Up to 10 feet (3m). Vigorous, upright growth; disease-resistant but poor winter hardiness. Leaves are glossy, dark green.

FLOWERS: Yellow changing to red, double, up to 3½ inches (9cm) across, borne in clusters, with red and yellow flowers in the same cluster. Mostly spring-flowering with sporadic repeat bloom. Similar to Circus but with stronger color tones and larger flowers. Slight fragrance.

USES: Especially beautiful trained along low fences.

JUST JOEY

TYPE: Hybrid tea

ORIGIN: Hybridized by Cants of Colchester (England) in 1972. A cross between Fragrant Cloud and Dr. A. J. Verhage.

RATING: ARS 8.0.

HABIT: Up to 6 feet (1.8m). Vigorous, upright, branching growth. Thorny canes bear large, leathery, glossy, dark green leaves.

FLOWERS: Buff orange, up to 6 inches (13cm) across. Very fragrant.

USES: Good centerpiece in mixed island beds. Long, strong stems are excellent for cutting. Needs cool summers and abundant moisture to grow well.

KABUKI (GOLDEN PRINCE)

TYPE: Hybrid tea

ORIGIN: Developed by the House of Meilland (France) and introduced by Universal Rose Selections (France) and Conard-Pyle (U.S.A.) in 1968. A cross between Carlo and Bettina with Peace and Soraya.

RATING: Not rated by the American Rose Society.

HABIT: 4 feet (1.2m). Vigorous, upright growth. Leaves are leathery, glossy, bronze.

FLOWERS: Deep yellow, double with 45 petals, high-centered in the mature bud stage. Pleasantly fragrant.

USES: Beds and borders. Excellent for cutting.

KING'S RANSOM

TYPE: Hybrid tea

ORIGIN: Developed by Dr. D. Morey (U.S.A.) and introduced by Jackson & Perkins (U.S.A.) in 1961. A cross between Gold Masterpiece and Lydia.

RATING: ARS 6.7. All-America Award 1962.

HABIT: 3 to 4 feet (.9 to 1.2m). Vigorous, strong, erect growth; hardy. Leaves are leathery, glossy, dark green.

FLOWERS: Golden yellow with pink tinge to the petal tips, up to 5 inches (13cm) across. Moderately fragrant.

USES: The lower petals tend to curl under, giving the flowers a distinctive appearance admired by floral arrangers. Good for massed bedding and cutting gardens.

LADY

TYPE: Hybrid tea

ORIGIN: Hybridized and introduced by the the House of Weeks (U.S.A.) in 1984. A cross between Song of Paris and Royal Highness.

RATING: ARS 7.0.

HABIT: 3 to 4 feet (.9 to 1.2m). Upright, compact growth. Leaves are large, medium green.

FLOWERS: Pink, double with 35 petals, up to 4½ inches (11.5cm) across. Slight fragrance.

USES: Beds and borders. The clear pink flowers are enchanting in floral arrangements, especially in the mature bud stage.

LADY X

TYPE: Hybrid tea

ORIGIN: Hybridized by the House of Meilland (France) and introduced by Conard-Pyle (U.S.A.) in 1966. A cross between Simone and an unnamed seedling.

RATING: ARS 8.3.

HABIT: 4 feet (1.2m). Vigorous, upright growth. Leaves are leathery, dark green.

FLOWERS: Mauve, double, high-centered, up to 5 inches (13cm) across. Lightly fragrant.

USES: Beds and borders. Combines well with yellow-flowered hybrid teas.

LA REINE VICTORIA

TYPE: Old garden rose

ORIGIN: Developed by J. Schwartz (France) in 1872. Derived from crosses between China roses and Damask roses. Classified as a Bourbon rose.

RATING: ARS 7.7 (actually deserving of a much higher rating). Probably the most popular of all old garden roses.

HABIT: Up to 6 feet (1.8m). Upright, spreading growth; hardy and disease-resistant. Thorny canes bear semiglossy, light green leaves.

FLOWERS: Shell-pink, double-cupped, 3 inches (7.5cm) across; resembles poppy or ranunculus. Prolific flowering in late spring. Wonderful apple fragrance.

USES: Best trained on a wide trellis or high fence with the canes splayed out like a fan. A true, old-fashioned look and aroma highly prized by floral arrangers.

LAS VEGAS

TYPE: Hybrid tea

ORIGIN: Hybridized by the House of Kordes (Germany) in 1981. Resulting from a cross between Ludwigshafen am Rhein and Feuerzauber.

RATING: ARS 7.5. Gold Medal Geneva 1985.

HABIT: 4 feet (1.2m). Vigorous, upright, bushy growth. Leaves are glossy, medium green.

FLOWERS: Deep orange, lighter orange on reverse; double with 26 petals, borne singly or in clusters of up to three. Individual blooms measure up to 5 inches (13cm) across. Pleasant fragrance.

USES: Beds and borders. Combines well with lavender-blue roses, such as Angel Face and Blue Moon.

LOVE

TYPE: Grandiflora

ORIGIN: Hybridized by William Warriner (U.S.A.) and introduced by Jackson & Perkins (U.S.A.) in 1980. A cross between Redgold and an unnamed seedling.

RATING: ARS 7.5. All-America Rose Selection 1980.

HABIT: 3 to 4 feet (.9 to 1.2m). Bushy growth. Leaves are dark glossy green.

FLOWERS: Magenta-red with silvery white underside, fully double, high-centered. Up to 4 inches (10cm) across, especially beautiful in the mature bud stage when the two-tone coloring is most noticeable. Slight fragrance.

USES: Good for massing. Superb for cutting; exhibition quality. Introduced as an award-winning trio with Cherish (coral-pink florabunda) and Honor (white hybrid tea).

MADAME HARDY

TYPE: Old garden rose

ORIGIN: Introduced in 1832 by an English rose grower named Hardy. Classified as a Damask.

RATING: ARS 8.8 (a phenomenally high rating for an old-fashioned rose).

HABIT: Up to 6 feet (1.8m). Vigorous, bushy, dense growth; hardy and disease-resistant. Leaves are gray-green.

FLOWERS: Snow white with a green tint in the center, double, flat, up to 3½ inches (9cm) across. Blooms in one spectacular, flowery avalanche in early summer. Sweet fragrance.

USES: The most popular old-fashioned white rose. A spectacular accent in mixed beds and borders, planted against old walls, and in informal cottage-style gardens. Prune after flowering to maintain vigor.

MADRAS

TYPE: Hybrid tea

ORIGIN: Hybridized by William Warriner (U.S.A.) and introduced by Jackson & Perkins (U.S.A.) in 1981. Resulting from crosses between unnamed seedlings.

RATING: Not rated by the American Rose Society.

HABIT: 4 feet (1.2m). Bushy, spreading growth. Leaves are large, medium green, leathery. Thorns are hooked downward on canes.

FLOWERS: Rich rose-pink with yellow and lighter pink reverse, fully double with 48 petals, up to 4½ inches (11.5cm) across. Fragrant.

USES: Beds and borders. Attractive in the mature bud stage as a cut flower.

MAGIC CAROUSEL

TYPE: Miniature

ORIGIN: Hybridized by R. S. Moore (U.S.A.) and introduced by Sequoia Nurseries (U.S.A.) in 1972. A cross between Little Darling and Westmont.

RATING: ARS 9.1. Award of Excellence American Rose Society 1975.

HABIT: Up to 2 feet (.6m). Dwarf, compact, branching growth; hardy and disease-resistant. Leaves are semiglossy, medium green.

FLOWERS: White with red petal tips, semidouble, up to 1¾ inches (4.5cm) across. No fragrance.

USES: Massing in beds and borders, especially mixed with other miniatures. Popular for containers and edging.

MARINA

TYPE: Floribunda

ORIGIN: Hybridized and introduced by the House of Kordes (Germany) in 1974. A cross between Color Wonder and an unnamed seedling.

RATING: ARS 8.0. All-America Award 1981.

HABIT: Up to 4 feet (1.2m). Erect, branching growth. Leaves are leathery, glossy, dark green.

FLOWERS: Orange, double, up to 3 inches (7.5cm) across, borne in clusters. Slight fragrance.

USES: Exquisite cut flower; in the mature bud stage, the high, pointed blooms are beautiful as sweetheart roses.

MARY ROSE

TYPE: Shrub rose

ORIGIN: Hybridized and introduced by David Austin (Great Britain) in 1983. A cross between The Friar and an unnamed seedling.

RATING: Not rated by the American Rose Society.

HABIT: Up to 5 feet (1.5m). Vigorous, bushy growth. Leaves are medium-size, medium green.

FLOWERS: Pink, fully double, up to 4 inches (10cm) across. Resemble old-fashioned cupped shrub roses, but bloom recurrently. Highly fragrant.

USES: Good accent for beds and borders; suitable for informal hedging.

MATANGI

TYPE: Floribunda

ORIGIN: Hybridized and introduced by the House of McGredy (New Zealand) in 1974. The result of crossing Picasso and an unnamed seedling. Sometimes misspelled Matonga.

RATING: ARS 7.0. Gold Medals, Britain 1974, Rome 1974, Belfast 1976.

HABIT: 3 to 4 feet (.9 to 1.2m). Bushy. Leaves are small, dark green.

FLOWERS: Orange-red with silvery petal centers and reverse, 30 petals, up to 3½ inches (9cm) across, borne in clusters. Slightly fragrant.

USES: Massing in beds and borders; low hedging.

MEDALLION

TYPE: Hybrid tea

ORIGIN: Hybridized by William Warriner (U.S.A.) and introduced by Jackson & Perkins (U.S.A.) in 1973. A cross between South Seas and King's Ransom.

RATING: ARS 7.6. All-America Award 1973.

HABIT: Up to 4 feet (1.2m). Vigorous, erect, branching growth; hardy and disease-resistant. Leaves are large, dark green.

FLOWERS: Pale apricot, double, huge, up to 8 inches (20cm) across. Fruity aroma.

USES: Dramatic highlight; tends to produce its best floral display in autumn. The long, graceful buds are popular with floral arrangers.

MEIDOMONAC (BONICA '82)

TYPE: Shrub rose

ORIGIN: Hybridized and introduced by the House of Meilland (France) in 1981, introduced by Conard-Pyle (U.S.A.) in 1987. A cross between a seedling of *Rosa sempervirens* and Mlle. Marthe Carron onto Picasso. A member of the Meidiland family of landscape roses.

RATING: ARS 8.0. All-America Award 1987.

HABIT: Up to 5 feet (1.5m). Bushy, spreading growth; hardy and disease-resistant. Leaves are small, glossy, dark green.

FLOWERS: Light pink, double, ruffled petals, up to 3½ inches (9cm) across. Everblooming from late spring to autumn frost. Lightly scented.

USES: Most often a slope cover.

MERCEDES GALLART

TYPE: Climbing hybrid tea

ORIGIN: Hybridized by B. Munne (France) and introduced by Jackson & Perkins (U.S.A.) in 1932. A cross between Souvenir de Claudius Denoyel and Souvenir de Claudius Pernet.

RATING: Not rated by the American Rose Society.

HABIT: Up to 15 feet (4.6m). Vigorous, long, hardy canes bear glossy, dark green leaves.

FLOWERS: Deep pink, fully double, up to 4½ inches (11cm) across. Spectacularly large for a climber. Some recurrent bloom after a beautiful late spring display. Highly fragrant.

USES: Training up trellis to cover arbors.

MILESTONE

TYPE: Hybrid tea

ORIGIN: Hybridized by William Warriner (U.S.A.) and introduced by Jackson & Perkins (U.S.A.) in 1985. A cross between Sunfire and Spellbinder.

RATING: ARS 7.9.

HABIT: 4 feet (1.2m). Upright growth. Leaves are large, semiglossy, medium green.

FLOWERS: Red with silvery red reverse, opening to coral-pink; double with 40 petals, cupped, up to 5 inches (13cm) across. Good repeat bloom, especially in autumn. Slightly fragrant.

USES: Beds and borders; eye-catching in the garden. Good for cutting.

MINT JULEP

TYPE: Hybrid tea

ORIGIN: Hybridized and introduced by Armstrong Roses (U.S.A.) in 1983. A cross between White Masterpiece and Queen Elizabeth.

RATING: Not rated by the American Rose Society.

HABIT: 4 feet (1.2m). Upright growth. Leaves are semiglossy, medium green.

FLOWERS: Pale green blending to pink, double with 35 petals, up to 4½ inches (11.5cm) across. Slight fragrance.

USES: Beds and borders. Exquisite cut flower.

MISS ALL-AMERICAN BEAUTY

TYPE: Hybrid tea

ORIGIN: Developed by the House of Meilland (France) and introduced in North America by Conard-Pyle (U.S.A.) in 1967. A cross between Chrysler Imperial and Karl Herbst. Often confused with the old garden rose American Beauty.

RATING: ARS 8.7. All-America Award 1968.

HABIT: Up to 4 feet (1.2m); a climbing form reaches up to 8 feet (2.4m) high. Hardy and disease-resistant. Leaves are leathery, medium green.

FLOWERS: Deep pink, fully double, high-centered, up to 5 inches (13cm) across. Good fragrance.

USES: Massing in beds and borders. Exquisite cut flower.

MISTER LINCOLN

TYPE: Hybrid tea

ORIGIN: Hybridized by Swim & Weeks (U.S.A.) and introduced by Conard-Pyle (U.S.A.) in 1964. A cross between Chrysler Imperial and Charles Mallerin.

RATING: ARS 8.7. All-America Award 1965.

HABIT: Up to 5 feet (1.5m). Erect, branching growth. Leaves are large, leathery, dark green.

FLOWERS: Dark red, double, up to 6 inches (15cm) across. Heavily fragrant, velvety texture.

USES: Good accent in beds and borders. The high, pointed buds are treasured by floral arrangers.

MON CHERIE

TYPE: Hybrid tea

ORIGIN: Hybridized and introduced by Armstrong Roses (U.S.A.) in 1981. A cross between White Satin and Bewitcned with Double Delight.

RATING: ARS 7.6. All-America Rose Selection 1981.

HABIT: 4 feet (1.2m). Upright growth. Leaves are semiglossy, medium green.

FLOWERS: Clear pink blending to yellow at center, maturing to dark red, double with 38 petals; most blooms borne singly, but some in clusters of up to three blooms. Individual flowers measure up to 4½ inches (11.5cm) across. Lightly fragrant.

USES: Good accent in mixed beds and borders. Popular for cutting.

NEVADA

TYPE: Shrub rose

ORIGIN: Hybridized and introduced by Pedro Dot (Spain) in 1927. A hybrid between La Giralda and *R. moyesii*. Classified as hybrid Moyesii.

RATING: ARS 8.2.

HABIT: Up to 8 feet (2.4m). Tall, erect, bushy growth; hardy and disease-resistant. Thorny canes bear small, glossy, green leaves.

FLOWERS: Pure white, conspicuous crown of yellow stamens, single, up to 5 inches (13cm) across. No fragrance.

USES: Wonderful accent in informal cottage-style gardens. Sensational trained along stair and bridge rails, on fences, and up trellis.

NEW DAWN

TYPE: Climbing rose

ORIGIN: Discovered by Somerset Rose Nursery (Great Britain) and introduced by Dreer (U.S.A.) in 1930. An everblooming sport of Dr. W. Van Fleet. The world's first patented flowering plant.

RATING: ARS 7.1.

HABIT: Up to 15 feet (4.6m). Vigorous, upright growth; hardy and disease-resistant. Leaves are glossy, leathery, dark green.

FLOWERS: Pink, double, up to 4 inches (10cm) across, borne in clusters. Repeat blooming. Good fragrance.

USES: Training up trellis, over arbors, along walls.

NURIA DE RECOLONS

TYPE: Old garden rose

ORIGIN: Developed by Pedro Dot (Spain) and introduced in 1933. A cross between Canigo and Frau Karl Druschki. Classified as a hybrid perpetual.

RATING: Not rated by the American Rose Society.

HABIT: Bushy growth, up to 6 feet (1.8m) high. Arching canes bear dense, semiglossy, medium green leaves.

FLOWERS: White, double, up to 4 inches (10cm) across, borne in clusters. Slightly fragrant.

USES: Best used as a background to perennial borders. A collector's item mostly seen in old rose collections.

OKLAHOMA

TYPE: Hybrid tea

ORIGIN: Hybridized and introduced by the House of Weeks (U.S.A.) in 1964. A cross between Chrysler Imperial and Charles Mallerin.

RATING: ARS 6.0. Gold Medal Japan 1963.

HABIT: 4 feet (1.2m); climbing Oklahoma grows to 8 feet (2.4m). Vigorous, bushy growth. Leaves are leathery, dark green.

FLOWERS: Dark red, double with 48 petals, high-centered, large, up to 5½ inches (14cm) across. Very fragrant.

USES: Beds and borders. Popular for potpourri. Excellent for cutting, especially in the mature bud stage. Climbing form is suitable for training up trellis.

OLÉ

TYPE: Grandiflora

ORIGIN: Hybridized and introduced by Armstrong Roses (U.S.A.) in 1964. A cross between Roundelay and El Capitan.

RATING: ARS 7.5.

HABIT: 4 to 5 feet (1.2 to 1.5m); climbing form reaches 8 feet (2.4m). Vigorous, upright growth. Leaves are glossy, dark green.

FLOWERS: Orange-red, double with 50 petals, high-centered, up to 6 inches (15cm) across. Fragrant.

USES: Beds and borders. Climbing form is suitable for training up trellis but not so highly rated.

OLYMPIAD

TYPE: Hybrid tea

ORIGIN: Hybridized by the House of McGredy (New Zealand) and introduced by Armstrong Roses (U.S.A.) in 1984. A cross between Red Planet and Pharaoh.

RATING: ARS 8.1. All-America Award 1984; official rose of the 1984 Olympic Games.

HABIT: Up to 5 feet (1.5m). Vigorous, erect, branching growth; hardy and disease-resistant. Leaves are medium size, medium green.

FLOWERS: Deep red, double, high-centered, up to 5 inches (13cm) across. Similar to Mister Lincoln, but generally better exhibition quality and more free-flowering, not as fragrant.

USES: Massing in beds and borders.

ORANGE HONEY

TYPE: Miniature

ORIGIN: Hybridized by R. S. Moore (U.S.A.) and introduced by Sequoia Nurseries (U.S.A.) in 1979. A cross between Rumba and Over the Rainbow.

RATING: ARS 7.9.

HABIT: Up to 12 inches (31cm). Dwarf, bushy, compact growth. Leaves are small, matt green.

FLOWERS: Bright orange fading to pink, semidouble, up to 1½ inches (4cm) across. Light fruity fragrance.

USES: Excellent for hanging baskets, pots, edging beds and borders.

OREGOLD

TYPE: Hybrid tea

ORIGIN: Hybridized by the House of Tantau (Germany) and introduced by Jackson & Perkins (U.S.A.) in 1975. A cross between Piccadilly and Colour Wonder (Konigin der Rosen).

RATING: ARS 7.5. All-America Award 1975.

HABIT: Up to 4 feet (1.2m). Vigorous, erect, branching growth; disease-resistant. Leaves are glossy, dark green.

FLOWERS: Deep golden yellow, double, up to 6 inches (15cm) across. Lightly fragrant.

USES: Good accent in mixed beds and borders. Extremely popular in cool coastal locations. Needs protection where winters are severe.

PAINTER RENOIR

TYPE: Old garden rose

ORIGIN: A hybrid shrub rose named for the painter Renoir, who loved roses. Hybridized by Henri Estable (France) in 1911 and reintroduced in 1992 from cuttings taken from the artist's garden near Nice. Not to be confused with a modern fragrant pink hybrid tea, Auguste Renoir, introduced by Meilland (France) in the same year.

RATING: Not rated by the American Rose Society. Gold Medal Nice Horticultural Society.

HABIT: Up to 6 feet (1.8m). Long, arching, thorny canes can create a bushy form or be trained to climb up trellis; hardy and heat-resistant. Leaves are small, dark green.

FLOWERS: Pale pink, double, up to 4 inches (10cm) across. Blooms in late spring. Slight fragrance.

USES: Training up pedestals and trellis, draping over walls and fences.

PARADISE

TYPE: Hybrid tea

ORIGIN: Hybridized by the House of Weeks (U.S.A.) and introduced by Conard-Pyle (U.S.A.) in 1978. A cross between Swarthmore and an unnamed seedling.

RATING: ARS 8.5. All-America Award 1979.

HABIT: Up to 4 feet (1.2m). Vigorous, erect, compact, branching growth; disease-resistant. Leaves are dull green.

FLOWERS: Light pink with petal tips edged in deep pink, double, up to 5 inches (13cm) across. Petals seem to swirl, especially in the mature bud stages.

USES: Beloved by floral arrangers because of its romantic bicolor hues.

PASCALI

TYPE: Hybrid tea

ORIGIN: Hybridized by L. Lens (Belgium) and A. Dickson (Ireland) in 1963 and introduced by Armstrong Roses (U.S.A.) in 1968. A cross between Queen Elizabeth and White Butterfly.

RATING: ARS 8.4. All-America Award 1969; Gold Medals, Portland 1967, The Hague 1963.

HABIT: Up to 4 feet (1.2m). Vigorous, erect, bushy, compact. One of the best mildew-resistant whites. Strong canes bear dark green leaves.

FLOWERS: White with a peachy glow at the center, double, high-centered, up to 4½ inches (11.5cm) across. Slightly fragrant.

USES: Massing in beds and borders. Exquisite cut flower that combines especially well with Royal Highness and Queen Elizabeth in floral arrangements.

PAUL'S SCARLET CLIMBER

TYPE: Climbing rose

ORIGIN: Hybridized by W. Paul (Great Britain) in 1916. A cross between Paul's Carmine Pillar and Reve d'Or.

RATING: ARS 7.7. Gold Medal Royal National Rose Society 1915, Gold Medal Bagatelle 1918.

HABIT: Up to 15 feet (4.6m). Vigorous, hardy canes bear glossy, dark green leaves.

FLOWERS: Scarlet, semidouble, up to 2½ inches (6.5cm) across, borne in dense clusters. Extremely free-flowering; the main display is concentrated in late spring. Similar in appearance to Blaze, which was first introduced under the name Improved Paul's Scarlet. Slightly fragrant.

USES: Excellent for training along fence rails and up trellis. Suitable for covering arbors.

PEACE

TYPE: Hybrid tea

ORIGIN: Hybridized by the House of Meilland (France) and introduced by Conard-Pyle (U.S.A.) in 1945. A complicated cross involving Margaret McGredy as one parent and a seedling from numerous crosses as the other parent.

RATING: ARS 8.5. All-America Award 1946; many other international awards. One of North America's most popular roses.

HABIT: Up to 6 feet (1.8m). Climbing Peace grows taller. Vigorous, erect, branching growth; hardy and disease-resistant. Leaves are glossy, dark green.

FLOWERS: Light yellow with a blush of pink at the petal edges, double, up to 6 inches (15cm) across. Slightly fragrant.

USES: Good garden accent, massing in beds and borders.

PERFUME DELIGHT

TYPE: Hybrid tea

ORIGIN: Hybridized by the House of Weeks (U.S.A.) and introduced by Conard-Pyle (U.S.A.) in 1973. A complicated cross involving Chrysler Imperial and Peace as the main parents.

RATING: ARS 7.7. All-America Award 1974.

HABIT: Up to 4 feet (1.2m). Bushy, branching habit. Leaves are large, leathery, dull green.

FLOWERS: Deep pink, double, up to 5 inches (13cm) across. Spicy old rose fragrance.

USES: Good accent in fragrance gardens. Good for cutting.

PERMANENT WAVE

TYPE: Floribunda

ORIGIN: Hybridized by M. Leenders (Holland) in 1932 and introduced by Jackson & Perkins (U.S.A.) in 1935. A sport of Else Poulsen. Also known as Duchess of Windsor.

RATING: ARS 7.5. Gold Medals, Bagatelle 1933, Rome 1934.

HABIT: 4 feet (1.2m). Vigorous, bushy growth. Leaves are glossy, dark green.

FLOWERS: Carmine-red, semidouble, wavy petals, up to 3 inches (7.5cm) across, borne in clusters. Slightly fragrant.

USES: Beds and borders. Good highlight for perennial borders, especially planted against old stone walls and rustic fences.

PHARAOH

TYPE: Hybrid tea

ORIGIN: Hybridized by the House of Meilland (France) and Universal Rose Selections (France) in 1967 and introduced by Conard-Pyle (U.S.A.) in 1969. A cross between Happiness and Independence with Suspense.

RATING: ARS 7.5. Gold Medals, Madrid 1961, Geneva 1967, The Hague 1967, Belfast 1969.

HABIT: 4 feet (1.2m). Upright growth. Leaves are leathery, glossy, dark green.

FLOWERS: Orange-red, high-centered, large, up to 5 inches (13cm) across. Fragrant.

USES: Beds and borders. Attractive cut flower, especially in the mature bud stage.

PINATA

TYPE: Climbing rose

ORIGIN: Hybridized by S. Suzuki (Japan) and introduced by Jackson & Perkins (U.S.A.) in 1978. A cross between seedlings of unknown parents.

RATING: ARS 7.0.

HABIT: Up to 8 feet (2.4m). Climbing habit. Hardy canes bear semiglossy leaves.

FLOWERS: Yellow with orange petal edges, double, up to 3 inches (7.5cm) across. Prolific flowering in cool weather. Slightly fragrant.

USES: Sensational trained up trellis and along low fences.

PINK MEIDILAND

TYPE: Shrub rose

ORIGIN: Developed and introduced by the House of Meilland (France) in 1983. A cross between Anne de Bretagne and Nirvana.

RATING: ARS 8.1.

HABIT: Up to 5 feet (1.5m). Vigorous, bushy growth; hardy and disease-resistant. Leaves are leathery, green.

FLOWERS: Deep pink with a white eye surrounding a ring of stamens, single, five-petaled, up to 2½ inches (6.5cm) across. Extremely free-flowering from late spring until autumn frost. No fragrance.

USES: Covering problem slopes, training along split rail fences. Makes a good informal hedge and windbreak. One of a large family of landscape roses called Meidilands. Colors include crimson, white, red, pink.

PINK PEACE

TYPE: Hybrid tea

ORIGIN: Hybridized by the House of Meilland (France) and introduced by Universal Rose Selections (France) and Conard-Pyle (U.S.A.) in 1959. A cross between Peace and Monique onto Peace and Mrs. John Lang.

RATING: ARS 7.7. All-America Award 1974; Gold Medals, Geneva 1959, Rome 1959.

HABIT: Up to 5 feet (1.5m). Vigorous, erect, branching growth. Leaves are leathery, blue-green.

FLOWERS: Deep rose-pink, double, high-centered, up to 6 inches (15cm) across. Uplifting old rose fragrance.

USES: Excellent for massing in a bed and for cutting.

POPCORN

TYPE: Miniature

ORIGIN: Hybridized by Dr. D. Morey (U.S.A.) and introduced by Pixie Treasures Miniature Roses (U.S.A.) in 1973. A cross between Katharina Zeimet and Diamond Jewel.

RATING: ARS 8.0.

HABIT: Up to 2½ feet (.8m). Vigorous, spreading, arching growth. Leaves are small, rich green, glossy.

FLOWERS: Pure white, semidouble, up to 1 inch (2.5cm) across, borne in dense clusters of up to 25 blooms. Buttery yellow stamens at the center of each flower give the appearance of a cascade of popcorn. Slight honey fragrance.

USES: Most effective grafted to a tall, straight rose stem to create a beautiful tree-form standard for planting in a container.

PRIMA DONNA

TYPE: Hybrid tea

ORIGIN: Hybridized by Takeshi Shirakawa (Japan) and introduced by Tosh Nakashima Nursery (U.S.A.) in 1983. Resulting from a cross between Happiness with Prominent and an unnamed seedling.

RATING: ARS 7.7. All-America Rose Selection 1988.

HABIT: 4 feet (1.2m). Bushy, spreading growth. Leaves are large, semiglossy, medium green.

FLOWERS: Deep fuchsia-pink, large, fully double with 27 petals, up to 5 inches (13cm) across. Slight fragrance.

USES: Though popular for garden display in beds and borders, it is also grown as a greenhouse variety for the cut-flower industry. Exhibition quality.

PRINCESS DE MONACO

TYPE: Hybrid tea

ORIGIN: Hybridized and introduced by the House of Meilland (France) in 1981. A cross between Ambassador and Peace. Also known as Grace Kelly.

RATING: ARS 7.2.

HABIT: 4 feet (1.2m). Upright, bushy growth. Leaves are large, glossy, dark green.

FLOWERS: Creamy white edged with pink, high-centered, double with 35 petals, up to 5 inches (13cm) across. Fragrant.

USES: Beds and borders. Exquisite cut flower in the mature bud stage. Exhibition quality.

PRISTINE

TYPE: Hybrid tea

ORIGIN: Developed by William Warriner (U.S.A.) and introduced by Jackson & Perkins (U.S.A.) in 1978. A cross between White Masterpiece and First Prize.

RATING: ARS 8.0.

HABIT: Up to 4 feet (1.2m). Erect, branching growth; disease-resistant. Leaves are glossy, reddish-green.

FLOWERS: Ivory-white with a hint of pink at the petal edges and a blush of golden yellow towards the petal base, surrounding a deep orange cluster of stamens when fully open. Up to 6 inches (15cm) across. Slight fragrance.

USES: Admired by flower arrangers, who like the high, pointed flower form in its mature bud stage.

PROMINENT

TYPE: Grandiflora

ORIGIN: Hybridized and introduced by the House of Kordes (Germany) in 1971. A cross between Colour Wonder and Zorina.

RATING: ARS 7.0. All-America Rose Selection 1977; Gold Medal Portland 1977.

HABIT: 4 feet (1.2m). Upright growth. Leaves are dark green.

FLOWERS: Orange-red, double with 33 petals; the long, pointed buds open out to form a cup shape. Slightly fragrant.

USES: Beds and borders. Attractive cut flower.

PUPPY LOVE

TYPE: Miniature

ORIGIN: Hybridized by E. W. Schwartz (U.S.A.) and introduced in 1978 by Nor'east Miniature Roses (U.S.A.). A cross between Zorina and an unnamed seedling.

RATING: ARS 8.6. Award of Excellence American Rose Society 1979.

HABIT: Up to 12 inches (31cm). Dwarf, bushy, compact growth. Leaves are medium green.

FLOWERS: Orange, pink, and coral blend, double, high-centered, up to 1½ inches (4cm) across. Slightly fragrant.

USES: Flowering pot plant, edging beds and borders, dainty floral arrangements. Exhibition quality.

PURITY

TYPE: Climbing rose

ORIGIN: Introduced by Hoopes, Brown & Thomas (Great Britain) in 1917. A cross between an unnamed seedling and Mme. Caroline Testout.

RATING: Not rated by the American Rose Society.

HABIT: Up to 15 feet (4.6m). Long, vigorous, thorny canes bear light green leaves.

FLOWERS: Pure white, semidouble, up to 4 inches (10cm) across. An avalanche of beautiful pristine blossoms in late spring. Slightly fragrant.

USES: Sensational trained over an arch. A superb component of "all-white" gardens.

QUEEN ELIZABETH

TYPE: Grandiflora

ORIGIN: Hybridized by Dr. W. E. Lammerts (U.S.A.) and introduced by Germain's Roses (U.S.A.) in 1954. A cross between Charlotte Armstrong and Floradora.

RATING: ARS 9.1. All-America Award 1955. One of North America's top-selling roses.

HABIT: Up to 6 feet (1.8m). Erect, branching habit. Almost thorn-free stems bear large, glossy, dark green leaves.

FLOWERS: Pale pink, double, high-centered, up to 4 inches (10cm) across, borne singly and in clusters. Slightly fragrant.

USES: Hedging, screen or tall background accent. Valued by floral arrangers; exquisite cut flower combines especially well with Pascali and Royal Highness in floral arrangements.

RED FOUNTAIN

TYPE: Climbing rose

ORIGIN: Hybridized by J. B. Williams (U.S.A.) and introduced by Conard-Pyle (U.S.A.) in 1975. A cross between Don Juan and Blaze.

RATING: ARS 7.4.

HABIT: Up to 15 feet (4.6m). Vigorous, long canes have the flower size of Don Juan and the free-flowering qualities of Blaze. Leaves are large, leathery, dark green.

FLOWERS: Scarlet-red, double, cupped, up to 4½ inches (11cm) across. Some repeat bloom. Good fragrance.

USES: Excellent for training up pillars and trellis.

RED MASTERPIECE

TYPE: Hybrid tea

ORIGIN: Hybridized by William Warriner (U.S.A.) and introduced by Jackson & Perkins (U.S.A.) in 1974. A complex cross involving Siren, Chrysler Imperial, and Carousel.

RATING: ARS 7.2.

HABIT: Up to 4 feet (1.2m). Vigorous, branching growth. Leaves are leathery, glossy, dark green, prone to mildew.

FLOWERS: Dark red, double, high-centered, up to 6 inches (15cm) across. Heavily fragrant.

USES: Garden display, cutting, potpourri.

REGENSBERG

TYPE: Floribunda

ORIGIN: Hybridized by William Warriner (U.S.A.) and introduced by Jackson & Perkins (U.S.A.) in 1974. A complex cross involving Siren, Chrysler Imperial, and Carousel.

RATING: ARS 8.0. Gold Medal Baden-Baden 1980.

HABIT: Up to 4 feet (1.2m). Low, bushy, branching growth. Leaves are attractive, blue-green.

FLOWERS: Rose-pink with white reverse and white petal edges, double, camellialike, 4½ inches (11cm) across. Old-fashioned, romantic appearance. Fragrant.

USES: Excellent for slope plantings; exquisite planted against old stone walls and barn siding.

REINE DES VIOLETTES (QUEEN OF THE VIOLETS)

TYPE: Old garden rose

ORIGIN: Introduced from France in 1860. Pius IX seedling. Classified as a hybrid perpetual.

RATING: Not rated by the American Rose Society.

HABIT: 5 to 6 feet (1.5 to 1.8m). Upright, bushy growth; hardy and disease-resistant. Pliable canes with few thorns bear small, medium green leaves.

FLOWERS: Mauve, fully double, up to 3 inches (7.5cm) across. Bloom heavily in spring, may repeat bloom in autumn. Highly fragrant.

USES: Beautiful trained up low trellis against walls and fences. Also potpourri, cutting

ROBIN HOOD

TYPE: Shrub rose

ORIGIN: Hybridized by Pemberton Roses (Great Britain) and introduced in 1927. A cross between Miss Edith Cavell and an unknown seedling. Classified as hybrid musk. Often listed as a hedge rose.

RATING: ARS 7.0.

HABIT: Up to 4½ feet (1.4m). Bushy, dense growth; hardy and disease-resistant. Thorny canes bear small, medium green leaves.

FLOWERS: Carmine-red to deep pink, semidouble, up to 1½ inches (4cm) across, borne in large clusters. Extremely prolific, late spring-flowering. No fragrance.

USES: Generally used as a flowering hedge, but also a good bushy accent in mixed beds and borders.

ROSA ALBA (WHITE ROSE OF YORK)

TYPE: Old garden rose

ORIGIN: One of several white roses commonly known as the Rose of York, famous as the emblem of the House of York in the War of the Roses. Origin unknown, probably Europe. Cultivated for centuries. A sport of *Rosa alba maxima*. Classified as Alba.

RATING: Not rated by the American Rose Society.

HABIT: Up to 8 feet (2.4m). Bushy, mounded growth; extremely hardy. Thorny canes bear dull green leaves.

FLOWERS: Pure white with conspicuous crown of yellow anthers in the middle, semidouble. Pleasant fragrance. Beautiful red hips are decorative in autumn.

USES: Informal gardens, especially where the plant can be allowed to spread.

ROSA BANKSIAE 'LUTEA' (LADY BANKS ROSE)

TYPE: Species rose

ORIGIN: Introduced from China.

RATING: ARS 9.0.

HABIT: 10 to 20 feet (3 to 6m), but can be kept bushy by heavy pruning. Vigorous, long canes are almost thorn-free. Leaves are small, light green. Grown mostly in mild-winter climates as a climber, since it is not reliably hardy.

FLOWERS: Yellow, double, 1 inch (2.5cm) across, borne in dense clusters in early spring. The white-flowered form is slightly fragrant.

USES: Training up trellis, over arbors, walls, fences. Combines well with azaleas and wisteria.

ROSA CANINA

TYPE: Dog rose

ORIGIN: Native to Europe, naturalized in North America. Cultivated prior to 1737.

RATING: Not rated by the American Rose Society.

HABIT: Up to 10 feet (3m). Vigorous, dense, mounded growth; hardy and disease-resistant. Leaves are dull, dark green.

FLOWERS: White or pale pink, single, up to 2 inches (5cm) across. No fragrance. Decorative scarlet hips cover the plants in autumn.

USES: Hedgerows and wildlife cover; edging meadows; windbreak. Roots are used as understock for grafting hybrids.

ROSA CAUDATA

TYPE: Species rose

ORIGIN: Introduced into cultivation from China about 1896.

RATING: Not rated by the American Rose Society.

HABIT: Up to 12 feet (3.7m). Upright, sprawling habit.

FLOWERS: Red, single, up to 2 inches (5cm) across, borne in clusters. Lightly fragrant.

USES: Suitable for climbing.

ROSA EGLANTERIA

TYPE: Species rose

ORIGIN: Native to Europe, especially England. Possibly cultivated prior to 1551. Known as the Sweet Brier rose.

RATING: ARS 7.7.

HABIT: Up to 8 feet (4.3m). Vigorous, bushy, dense growth. Hardy canes bear dark green leaves with an applelike fragrance.

FLOWERS: Pink, with a prominent circle of golden stamens at the center, single, five-petaled, up to 2 inches (5cm) across. Delicate, sweet fragrance.

USES: Excellent windbreak; good for hedgerows and wildlife cover. Naturalize throughout North America.

ROSA FOETIDA 'BICOLOR'

TYPE: Species rose

ORIGIN: A yellow-flowering single rose from Persia that has been cultivated in Europe for centuries. Commonly called the Austrian Copper rose, a natural sport of *R. foetida*.

RATING: ARS 8.1. The yellow form is rated 7.7.

HABIT: Up to 8 feet (2.4m). Erect, arching growth; not reliably hardy. Sparse thorny canes bear small, dull green leaves which invariably discolor from disease (usually black spot) and drop to the ground soon after the plant has bloomed in spring.

FLOWERS: Copper-red within, yellow reverse, with a conspicuous crown of yellow stamens, single, up to 2½ inches (6.5cm) across. An extraordinary color in roses. Fragrance is sickly sweet.

USES: Suitable for informal, cottage-style gardens.

ROSA GLAUCA (R. RUBRIFOLIA)

TYPE: Species rose

ORIGIN: Introduced from high elevation areas of Europe before 1830.

RATING: Not rated by the American Rose Society.

HABIT: 4 to 6 feet (1.2 to 1.8m). Bushy, fountainlike growth; hardy and disease-resistant. Arching canes are almost thornless, red. Leaves are small, serrated, dusky maroon.

FLOWERS: Pink, single, starlike, up to 1 inch (2.5cm) across, borne in small clusters. Spring-flowering. Fragrant.

USES: Good accent in informal gardens, especially combined with perennials. Mostly displayed as a curiosity in rose collections.

ROSA HUGONIS (FATHER HUGO'S ROSE)

TYPE: Species rose

ORIGIN: Introduced from China. Cultivated since 1899.

RATING: ARS 9.1.

HABIT: Up to 6 feet (1.8m). Bushy habit; moderately winter-hardy. Arching, thorny canes bear medium-size lustrous leaves. Prefers poor soil.

FLOWERS: Bright yellow, single, up to 2 inches (5cm) across. Extremely free-flowering in spring. No fragrance.

USES: Accent in mixed perennial and shrub borders. Suitable for rock gardens.

ROSA LAEVIGATA (CHEROKEE ROSE)

TYPE: Species rose

ORIGIN: Native to China, but widely naturalized throughout the southern United States, especially South Carolina and Georgia, where it has been adopted as the state flower.

RATING: ARS 7.0.

HABIT: Up to 20 feet (6m). Erect, rambling growth; not reliably hardy. Thorny canes hook onto rough surfaces and branches, climbing up the loftiest trees. Leaves are small, glossy, dark green, camellialike.

FLOWERS: White with a powdery yellow circle of stamens at the center, single, five-petaled, up to 5 inches (13cm) across. Spring-flowering. Gardenialike fragrance.

USES: Covering arbors, fences, trellis.

ROSA MOYESII (MOYES ROSE)

TYPE: Species rose

ORIGIN: Introduced to the Western world from China in 1903.

RATING: Not rated by the American Rose Society.

HABIT: Up to 13 feet (4m). Vigorous, bushy, mounded growth with a spread equal to its height; tough and hardy. Small, dull green leaves are arranged symmetrically on slender stems attached to thorny canes.

FLOWERS: Deep rose-red with a small circle of yellow stamens in the middle, single, cup-shaped, up to 2½ inches (6.5cm) across. Summer-flowering. Slightly fragrant.

USES: A good component of berry gardens, wild gardens, to mark property boundaries. Like the Multiflora rose, it makes an impenetrable hedge and highway barrier.

ROSA MULTIFLORA (MULTIFLORA ROSE)

TYPE: Species rose

ORIGIN: Introduced from China before 1868, now naturalized throughout North America and banned in many counties as an agricultural pest.

RATING: Not rated by the American Rose Society.

HABIT: Up to 12 feet (3.7m). Upright, bushy, aggressive habit; hardy and disease-resistant. Leaves are small, serrated, glossy, light green.

FLOWERS: Pure white, single, ¾ inch (2cm) across, borne in clusters. Summer-flowering. Small, round, orange-red hips are relished by songbirds. Slight fragrance.

USES: Hedging, windbreak, highway divider.

ROSA MUNDI

TYPE: Old garden rose

ORIGIN: Cultivated in gardens for hundreds of years. A sport of *R. gallica*, also called *R. gallica versicolor*.

RATING: Not rated by the American Rose Society.

HABIT: 3 to 4 feet (.9 to 1.2m). Bushy, upright growth; hardy and disease-resistant. Canes covered with bristles but few thorns bear coarse, dark green leaves.

FLOWERS: Semidouble, cup-shaped. Pink-and-white-striped, up to 3½ inches (9cm) across. Bloom early in the season. Fragrant.

USES: Low hedge, accent shrub; also potpourri.

ROSA POMIFERA

TYPE: Species rose

ORIGIN: Native to Europe and Asia; introduced into cultivation in 1771. Commonly called Apple rose for its large hips that have thick edible skins.

RATING: ARS 6.3.

HABIT: Up to 7 feet (2.1m); shrublike, mounded growth; hardy and disease-resistant. Thorny canes bear dark, dull green leaves.

FLOWERS: Pink fading to white in the center, single, up to 2 inches (5cm) across. Blooms early in spring. Fragrant.

USES: Good accent for edible landscapes. The decorative red hips can be peeled like an orange and eaten raw like an apple. Widely planted in American colonial gardens.

ROSA RUGOSA (RUGOSA ROSE)

TYPE: Species rose

ORIGIN: Introduced from northeastern Asia in 1845, it has made itself at home throughout North America, especially in coastal gardens.

RATING: Not rated by the American Rose Society.

HABIT: 4 to 5 feet (1.2 to 1.5m). Bushy, dense, spreading growth. Leaves are large, textured, glossy, dark green.

FLOWERS: Usually mauve, single, up to 3½ inches (9cm) across, but there are double forms and a pure white. Blooms continuously from late spring into autumn. Heavily fragrant. Produces large, decorative, scarlet hips, the skins of which are edible and rich in vitamin C.

USES: Hedging, windbreak, ground cover. Will grow on sand dunes and control soil erosion.

ROSA SERICEA PTERACANTHA (R. OMEIENSIS PTERACANTHA)

TYPE: Species rose

ORIGIN: From western China; introduced into cultivation in 1901. Commonly called Omei rose.

RATING: Not rated by the American Rose Society.

HABIT: Up to 6 feet (1.8m). Upright growth. The many triangular-shaped thorns are red, translucent. Young leaves are reddish green.

FLOWERS: White, single, up to 2 inches (5cm) across. Not fragrant.

USES: A connoisseur's plant. Grown for its ornamental stems rather than its flowers. Grown mostly as a winter accent since the brilliant red thorns glow when backlit by the sun.

ROSA WICHURAIANA (MEMORIAL ROSE)

TYPE: Species rose

ORIGIN: Introduced from eastern Asia in 1891 and used extensively in hybridizing climbing roses.

RATING: Not rated by the American Rose Society.

HABIT: 1 to 2 feet (.3 to .6m) as a ground cover; to 15 feet (4.6m) when trained to climb. Canes are thorny, hardy, disease-free. Leaves are medium-size, glossy, dark green.

FLOWERS: White, single, up to 2 inches (5cm) across, borne in clusters. Early summer-flowering. Fragrant.

USES: Ground cover. Climbing rose.

ROYAL HIGHNESS

TYPE: Hybrid tea

ORIGIN: Hybridized by Swim & Weeks (U.S.A.) and introduced by Conard-Pyle (U.S.A.) in 1962. A cross between Virgo and Peace.

RATING: ARS 8.5. All-America Award 1962; Gold Medals, Portland 1960, Madrid 1962; American Rose Society David Fuerstenberg Prize 1964.

HABIT: Up to 4 feet (1.2m). Low, bushy, compact growth. Leaves are leathery, dark green.

FLOWERS: Light shell-pink, double, high-centered, up to 5½ inches (14cm) across. Fine fragrance.

USES: Beautiful garden accent; exhibition quality. Exquisite cut flower, combines especially well with Pascali and Queen Elizabeth in floral arrangements.

SEA FOAM

TYPE: Shrub rose

ORIGIN: Hybridized by E. W. Schwartz (U.S.A.) and introduced by Conard-Pyle (U.S.A.) in 1964. A cross between seedlings of White Dawn and Pinocchio.

RATING: ARS 7.5. Gold Medal Rome 1963; American Rose Society David Fuerstenberg Prize 1968.

HABIT: Up to 12 feet (3.7m). Long, trailing, thorny canes can be left to sprawl like a ground cover or trained to climb. Leaves are small, glossy, dark green.

FLOWERS: Light pink fading to white, double, up to 2½ inches (6.5cm) across, borne in abundant clusters. Slightly fragrant.

USES: To drape over low stone walls and split rail fences and as a slope cover.

SCARLET KNIGHT

TYPE: Grandiflora

ORIGIN: Hybridized by the House of Meilland (France) in 1966 and introduced by Conard-Pyle (U.S.A.) in 1967. A cross between Happiness and Independence onto Sutter's Gold.

RATING: ARS 7.8. All-America Award 1966.

HABIT: Up to 6 feet (1.8m). Erect, branching growth; disease-resistant. Leaves are leathery, glossy, dark green.

FLOWERS: Scarlet, double, up to 4 inches (10cm) across, borne in clusters of two or three. Slightly fragrant, velvet texture.

USES: Good accent in mixed beds and borders. Superb for cutting.

SHOWBIZ

TYPE: Floribunda

ORIGIN: Hybridized by the House of Tantau (Germany) in 1981. Parents unknown, though obviously a cross involving other floribunda roses, one of which is probably a seedling of America for its fantastic bloom production, the other possibly a seedling of Dortmund for its color.

RATING: ARS 8.1. All-America Award 1985.

HABIT: Up to 4 feet (1.2m). Erect, bushy, compact growth. The glossy, dark green leaves are a perfect contrast to the deep red flowers.

FLOWERS: Blood-red, double, camellialike, up to 2½ inches (6.5cm) across, borne in large, dense clusters. No fragrance.

USES: Sensational for mass bedding. The strong flush of color in late spring and again in autumn is even more intense than a bed of red geraniums; shows good repeat bloom in between.

SHREVEPORT

TYPE: Grandiflora

ORIGIN: Hybridized by the House of Kordes (Germany) and introduced by Armstrong Roses (U.S.A.) in 1981. A cross between Zorina and Uwe Seeler. Named for the American Rose Society's test gardens in Alabama.

RATING: ARS 7.4. All-America Award 1982.

HABIT: Up to 5 feet (1.5m). Vigorous, erect, branching growth. Leaves are prickly, dark green.

FLOWERS: Orange and peach, double, up to 4 inches (10cm) across. Mild tea fragrance.

USES: Massing in beds and borders, especially as a background to low-growing floribundas.

SIMPLICITY

TYPE: Floribunda

ORIGIN: Hybridized by William Warriner (U.S.A.) and introduced by Jackson & Perkins (U.S.A.) in 1979. A cross between Iceberg and an unnamed seedling.

RATING: ARS 8.3. Gold Medal New Zealand 1976. One of North America's best-selling roses.

HABIT: Up to 5 feet (1.5m). Vigorous, erect, bushy growth; hardy and disease-resistant. Sometimes described as a shrub rose or hedge rose. Leaves are large, glossy, medium green.

FLOWERS: Shell-pink, semidouble, up to 4 inches (10cm) across, borne in clusters of four or five. Perpetual flowering. Slight fragrance.

USES: Hedging, screening, edging driveways, also planting in pairs at the entrance to homes.

STANWELL PERPETUAL

TYPE: Old garden rose

ORIGIN: A *Rosa spinosissima* hybrid introduced in 1838. Probably a cross between *R. damascena* 'Semperflorens' and *R. spinosissima*.

RATING: ARS 8.0.

HABIT: Up to 5 feet (1.5m). Vigorous, bushy, spreading growth; hardy and disease-resistant. Leaves are small, dark green.

FLOWERS: Light pink, double, up to 3½ inches (9cm) across. Early summer-flowering, some repeat bloom. Fragrant.

USES: Accent in informal cottage-style gardens and herb gardens.

STARINA

TYPE: Miniature

ORIGIN: Hybridized by the House of Meilland (France) and introduced by Conard-Pyle (U.S.A.) in 1965. A cross between Dany Robin and Fire King with Perla de Montserrat.

RATING: ARS 9.4 (the highest-rated miniature rose). Winner of more awards worldwide than any other miniature.

HABIT: Up to 1½ feet (.5m). Dwarf, bushy, compact growth. Leaves are glossy, dark green.

FLOWERS: Scarlet-red, double, up to 2 inches (5cm) across, borne singly and in clusters. No fragrance.

USES: Superb for edging beds and borders—creates a beautiful miniature flowering hedge. Superb pot plant; often sold as a flowering house plant.

SUMMER DAMASK (DAMASK ROSE)

TYPE: Old garden rose

ORIGIN: Introduced into European gardens from Damascus in the sixteenth century. Known botanically as *R. damascena*. The variety 'Kazanlik' is the source of the valuable oil used in perfumes known as attar of roses.

RATING: Not rated by the American Rose Society.

HABIT: Usually up to 5 feet (1.5m), but grows taller in rich soil. Bushy, spreading, arching growth. Leaves small, medium green. Requires rigorous pruning each winter.

FLOWERS: Usually white flushed with pink or red, up to 4 inches (10cm) across. Summer-blooming. Strong, pleasant fragrance. Flowers are followed by decorative, round, red hips.

USES: Popular accent in herb gardens, fragrance gardens. Valued for potpourri. More than 32,000 flowers are needed to produce 1 ounce (28 grams) of attar essence.

SUNDOWNER

TYPE: Grandiflora

ORIGIN: Hybridized by the House of McGredy (New Zealand) and introduced by Edmunds (U.S.A.) in 1978. A cross between Bond Street and Peer Gynt.

RATING: ARS 7.5. All-America Award 1979.

HABIT: Up to 5 feet (1.5m). Vigorous, erect canes are hardy and blackspot-resistant, but mildew-susceptible. Leaves are large, glossy, dark green with a coppery sheen.

FLOWERS: Glowing orange, double, up to 4 inches (10cm) across. Rich, spicy aroma.

USES: Extremely popular in coastal gardens as a garden accent. Popular for cutting.

SUNNY MEILLANDINA (SUNBLAZE)

TYPE: Miniature

ORIGIN: Hybridized and introduced by the House of Meilland (France) in 1985. A cross between Sarabande and Moulin Rouge onto Zambra and Meikim.

RATING: Not rated by the American Rose Society.

HABIT: Up to 18 inches (4.6cm). Dwarf, bushy, compact habit. Hardy canes bear small, dark green leaves.

FLOWERS: Orange, double, up to 1½ inches (4cm) across. No fragrance.

USES: Edging beds and borders; containers and raised planters.

SUNSPRITE

TYPE: Floribunda

ORIGIN: Hybridized by the House of Kordes (Germany) and introduced by Jackson & Perkins (U.S.A.) in 1977. A cross between Spanish Sun and an unnamed seedling.

RATING: ARS 8.0. Gold Medal Baden-Baden 1972.

HABIT: Up to 4 feet (1.2m). Vigorous, erect, bushy growth. Leaves are attractive, deep green.

FLOWERS: Deep yellow, double, camellialike, up to 3 inches (7.5cm) across, borne in clusters of three or four. The fade-resistant flowers bloom continuously all summer until autumn frosts. Pleasant fragrance.

USES: Massing in beds and borders. Sunsprite, Impatient, and Vogue make a stunning combination.

SUTTER'S GOLD

TYPE: Hybrid tea

ORIGIN: Hybridized and introduced by Armstrong Roses (U.S.A.) in 1950. A cross between Charlotte Armstrong and Signora.

RATING: ARS 6.9. All-America Award 1950; Gold Medals, Portland 1946, Bagatelle 1948, Geneva 1949; James Alexander Gamble Rose Fragrance Medal 1966.

HABIT: Up to 4 feet (1.2m). Vigorous, erect, branching growth; disease-resistant. Leaves are leathery, dark green.

FLOWERS: Golden yellow with a tint of light pink at the petal edges, double, up to 5 inches (13cm) across. Fruity fragrance.

USES: Eye-catching alone or massed in a bed. Good cut flower in the mature bud stage.

THE FAIRY

TYPE: Polyantha

ORIGIN: Developed by Bentall (Great Britain) in 1932. A cross between Paul Crampel and Lady Gay.

RATING: ARS 8.7.

HABIT: 2 feet (.6m). Busy, dense, spreading growth; hardy and disease-resistant. Thorny canes bear medium-size, glossy, green leaves.

FLOWERS: Light pink, double, cupped, up to 1½ inches (4cm) across, borne in clusters. No fragrance.

USES: A good ground cover for difficult-to-plant slopes and to control soil erosion. Makes a good hedge if supported on wires to hold the canes off the ground.

TIFFANY

TYPE: Hybrid tea

ORIGIN: Hybridized by Robert V. Lindquist (U.S.A.) and introduced by the Howard Rose Company (U.S.A.) in 1954. A cross between Charlotte Armstrong and Girona.

RATING: ARS 8.4. All-America Award 1955; American Rose Society David Fuerstenberg Prize; James Alexander Gamble Rose Fragrance Award 1962.

HABIT: Up to 5 feet (1.5m). Hardy, vigorous, disease-resistant canes bear glossy, dark green foliage.

FLOWERS: Pink with yellow tints. Fully double, high-centered blooms measure up to 5 inches (13cm) across, appear all season. Good fragrance.

USES: Accent in mixed beds and borders; suitable for mass bedding.

TROPICANA

TYPE: Hybrid tea

ORIGIN: Hybridized by the House of Tantau (Germany) in 1960 and introduced by Jackson & Perkins (U.S.A.) in 1962. Parentage not recorded.

RATING: ARS 8.4. All-America Award 1963; Gold Medal American Rose Society 1967.

HABIT: Up to 5 feet (1.5m). Erect, branching growth. Leaves are glossy, dark green.

FLOWERS: Orange-red with iridescent petals, double, up to 5 inches (13cm) across. Strong, pleasant fragrance.

USES: Massing in beds and borders. Prolific, exhibition-quality flowers.

VOGUE

TYPE: Floribunda

ORIGIN: Hybridized by Eugene Boerner (U.S.A.) and introduced by Jackson & Perkins (U.S.A.) in 1951. A cross between Pinocchio and Crimson Glory.

RATING: ARS 7.5. All-America Award 1952; Gold Medals, Portland 1950, Geneva 1950.

HABIT: Up to 4 feet (1.2m). Erect, bushy growth. Leaves are glossy, blue-green.

FLOWERS: Coral-pink, double, up to 4½ inches (11cm) across, borne in dense clusters. Lightly fragrant.

USES: Excellent for mass bedding on account of its free-flowering habit. A good companion to Impatient and Showbiz, which appear to be red versions of Vogue.

WHITE LIGHTNIN'

TYPE: Grandiflora

ORIGIN: Hybridized and introduced by Armstrong Roses (U.S.A.) in 1980. A cross between Angel Face and Misty.

RATING: ARS 7.5. All-America Award 1981.

HABIT: Up to 4 feet (1.2m). Erect, bushy growth. Leaves are handsome, glossy, dark green.

FLOWERS: Pure white with a hint of cream in the middle, double, up to 4 inches (10cm) across, borne in clusters. Strong citruslike aroma.

USES: Massing in beds and borders. Magnificent cut flower.

WHITE MASTERPIECE

TYPE: Hybrid tea

ORIGIN: Hybridized by Eugene Boerner (U.S.A.) and introduced in 1969 by Jackson & Perkins (U.S.A.). Parentage not recorded.

RATING: ARS 7.6.

HABIT: Up to 4 feet (1.2m). Vigorous, bushy growth; hardy and disease-resistant. Leaves are glossy, dark green, help to accentuate the flowers.

FLOWERS: Creamy white, double, up to 6 inches (15cm) across. Sweet fragrance.

USES: Massing in beds and borders. Beautiful cut flower; exhibition quality.